Praise for:

Why Women Want What They Can't Have & Men Want What They Had After It's Gone!

"One of the best books I have read on the dynamics of relationships. Dr. Sacco examines the reasons why so many relationships fail. The root of the problem is societal expectations and tainted gender socialization. He offers hope to those of us who strive for contentment with our partners. A reading must for anyone who desires a healthy, well-balanced and satisfying relationship. Surely, that's everyone."

- Stephanie Nielsen, B.A., M.Ed.
School Teacher for 30 years

"As a professional working in the field of addictions and as a recovered alcoholic/addict, I applaud Dr. Sacco's work which addresses the core of most, if not all, addictions... Co-dependency!"

-Walter Pohl
Addictions Counselor, Renascent Centres

"As a relationship/marital counselor, I highly recommend Why Women Want What They Can't Have!

The book makes sense and provides explanations for why we choose who we choose and why relationships succeed or fail. If you want to know what makes women, men and even yourself tick, read this book as it can and will make a difference for how you look at others and relationships."

-Andrea Peterson, M.S.W.
Psychotherapist in Private Practice

"Wow, Peter Sacco does a great job explaining why women and men are the way they are. He sheds new light on the concept of relationships and reveals a different perspective for looking at men and women!"

-Daniel Rodrique
Film Producer, Maple Tree Productions

"Dr. Sacco, Excellent... excellent! That's how I would describe your book "Why Women Want What They Can't Have". Informingly presented and insightful. In my opinion, a book that should be a 'must read' for any relationship."

- Joe Mayer, Supervising ADR Editor for the hit movie "Pretty Woman"

"Fear used to totally control me. That was until one day a miracle happened, and I awoke to the truth that

I had choices. I chose to live by faith instead of fear. Gaining power over my life choices helped me to break the cycle of dependency in my life. This book is very insightful and definitely worth reading."

- **Diane Doneff,** Executive Director Women's Addiction Recovery Mediation, (W.A.R.M.)

"Insightful, very easy to read and not time consuming...The stuff women should know!"

- **Linda Pelligrino**, Host AM Buffalo, (appeared as guest on the show)

"Explains why women want change and why men are so resistant!"

- **Rhonda London**, Host Rhonda London Live Show, (appeared as guest on the show)

"Gender Wars? This book can help you understand why men and women are at crossroads!"

- **Cheryl Clock**, Reporter St. Catherines Standard, ON, (featured news story on relationships)

"Great at explaining why abused women stay in bad marriages...You think you can really change a man?"

-**Judy Kay**, Reporter Niagara Gazette, NY USA, (featured news story on relationships)

"Interesting...a man talking about what women want!"

- **Michael Coren,** Michael Coren Live, (appeared as guest on the show)

"A man with the answers about what women want..."

- **Michael Lansberg,** TSN's Off The Record, (appeared as guest on the show)

" A unique book which looks at how women and men look at the same situations differently"

- **Connie Smith**, Anchor CH 11 News, (appeared as guest on the show)

Why Women Want What They Can't Have

WHY SO MANY RELATIONSHIPS FAIL...

Published in the United States by Booklocker.com, Inc., Bangor, Maine.

Printed in the United States of America on acid-free paper.

Booklocker.com, Inc.
2011

First Edition

Why Women Want What They Can't Have

WHY SO MANY RELATIONSHIPS FAIL...

Peter Andrew Sacco, Ph.D.

ACKNOWLEDGEMENTS

I would like to dedicate this book to all the wonderful people I have met in my life; family, friends, colleagues, students, clients and serendipitous encounters who have had a lasting, positive, and profound influence on me. I would like to thank those people who trusted in me to open windows so the sunshine could fill my life when doors were closed.

A big thanks to all those other teachers that I had the chance to learn under and a big thanks to all the great teachers I have year in and year out... my students and clients!

Some of the most important people I would personally like to thank are: my parents, John and Bridget, my sisters Melanie and Lisa, my aunts Angeline and Mary, my uncle Jim, and my grandmother Julie.

I would also like to dedicate this book to three awesome people who have passed on: Janet Kennedy, Alan Kurthi and Joe Mayer. Thank you for being who you were!

Finally, I would like to thank all of the people who have chosen to read this book. I hope the information and insights in this book help you live a better life and find lasting and healthy relationships.

All the best!

TABLE OF CONTENTS

FORWARD

Why Women Want What They Can't Have is the revised version of the popular selling first version *Women Want What They Can't Have*. Why Women Want What They Can't Have is an informative book which provides insights into why gender differences exist and why they will continue to exist generation after generation. Perhaps one of the greatest negative side-effects of gender differences is the high prevalence of divorce and separation rates amongst couples which haunts our society. These varied differences precipitate, antagonize and facilitate problems in relationships. If we could only understand them better, turn them around into positives and restructure our understanding of relationships, we could perhaps facilitate longer-term, healthier relationships.

As a professional, I am often times asked, "Why do women keep attracting the wrong males or ones they are not compatible with?"..." Why do some men leave good marriages, only to come crawling back on their hands and knees?" Well, funny as it may seem, hindsight really is 20/20! If we knew what we did wrong before we actually did wrong, then we might not do wrong in the first place if we had the wisdom beforehand. Most people have experienced failed relationships and all of us have definitely experienced our fair share of rejection. It's what we do after the experience which matters most. If we take our failures and misfortunes in the past and reframe them as "life's lessons", then we will ensure we are striving for something positive. We will have our eye on the mark and not settle for something mediocre or short of the mark. And this is most true in our everyday relationships with others. If we strive to be our best selves and want to be around positive people who offer their best selves, the likelihood of missing the mark is greatly lessened!

This book delves into the heart of the problem: Societal expectations and tainted gender socialization. Furthermore, it examines why women continue to be superior in their androgynous qualities and why men are struggling to keep pace. Will men ever be capable of being like women in their abilities to become intimate and communicative creatures? Will women continue to tolerate the Twentieth Century values and expectations of men? Will the new millennium bring the two genders closer and bridge the gap for misunderstanding? How can you better tolerate change in a relationship? If you are going through change in your own life, how can you make it less threatening and intimidating for your partner? Why do you tolerate abuse or neglect in a relationship? How much is too much and when is it time to close the chapter on that part of your life?

We are all social creatures who were taught to love others and in return be loved! There is no greater gift in life than the gift of love. So many people take it for granted in relationships and wind up losing out on the greatest tribute anyone can pay to another human: LOVE! Friendships and relationships are worth maintaining and saving, especially when you love the other person and they love you.

We're here for a short, good time, but not a long time. I wrote this book with the hopes of helping people understand other people better. Women understanding men better. Men understanding women better. Parents understanding children better. Children understanding parents better. Cultures are becoming more sensitive to the needs and diversities of one another when it comes to communication and relationships.

I hope you will be able to take something from this book and apply it to your life to pass it on to someone who can make good use of it. I would also like to pay tribute to the great minds/authors who have done great work and research looking at relationships and communication, and who have been a great influence in my lecturing and writing. Some of which include: Jack Canfield, Mark Victor Hansen, Dr. Robert H. Schuller, John Gray, and Deborah Tannen.

CHAPTER ONE

AN INTRODUCTION

Sometimes I wonder if men and women really suit each other. Perhaps they should live next door and just visit now and then.

Katharine Hepburn

What do women really want? What do men really want? What does anyone really want? To sum it up in one word: happiness! Happiness is a feeling with many meanings for different people. In the world of relationships, happiness usually means feeling good about oneself and feeling good about the other person. Unfortunately, in today's world this occurs with less frequency.

I attended a singles dance recently to find out what women and men are really looking for. Singles filled out questionnaires describing who their ideal mate would be. The questionnaires were then collated into a computer and an hour later singles were given a list of potential matches, and they were to find one another using the numerical name tag they were assigned. The experience was very interesting. Many really believed they would find their "soul mates" at the dance. Their future confidants!

I spoke with many men and women at the dance and asked them why they would choose this type of forum to meet people. Most responded with the answer: loneliness. Many were there to fill the void left in their lives from previous failed relations and broken marriages. I asked both women and men what they really wanted in their "ideal" relationships. Women reported wanting a man whom they could relate to and who could reciprocate quality communication. Men reported similar qualities they sought in women, but several of the divorced men stated they wanted a woman who could stay the way they were when they initially met them. In essence, men wanted women who would not change, while women wanted men who were not afraid of change and capable of evolving and adapting to relationships.

Everyone is unique and different. When you throw together individual differences plus gender differences you wind up with a tossed salad of misunderstandings and misconceptions. Author John Gray provides exceptional examples of how men and women differ in his bestselling book, Men Are from Mars, Women Are from Venus. Likewise, author Deborah Tannen examined the differences in communication which exist between the sexes in her book, You Don't Understand Me. She shows how gender differences in communication can cause misunderstandings between men and women.

Why are the differences between women and men greater than the similarities? Women want what they can't have because men want what they already had! Do you want to know why men won't change while women welcome change with open arms? In the chapters to follow I will show you why men and women are the way they are. I will present the underlying reasons why many relationships fail today and will continue to fail into the millennium because women want what they can't have and men want what they already had. Before you dig into the upcoming chapters, make a self-examination of your own life. What kind of person are you? How did your parents treat you as a child and how much did it influence who you are today? Do you possess a lot of the same similarities personality-wise as your parents? Are you happy with who you are today? Are you satisfied in your relationships? If you could make changes in your life, what would they be?

If you are discontent with who you are today and you find that you keep experiencing problems in your personal relationships, there are several key points to keep in mind as you read this book:

1) You can't change the past!

2) You can only live in the present.

3) You can live now to shape your future.

4) You may be a product of the past, but you can become anyone or anything you want to become in the here and now.

5) If anything is going to be, it's up to you.

6) Yes, differences exist between men and women, just as they do for all human beings.

7) It is individual differences which make relationships worth the adventure.

8) No one's perfect, not you or anyone you meet.

9) Don't be too hard on yourself or others.

10) Life is an awesome gift for a short duration. Make the most of it and dare to dream!

CHAPTER TWO

WOMEN WANT WHAT THEY CAN'T HAVE: FOR MEN TO BE LIKE THEM

Once the realization is accepted that even between the closest human beings infinite distances continue to exist, a wonderful living side by side can grow up, if they succeed in loving the distance between them which makes it possible for each to see each other whole against the sky.

Rainer Maria Rilke

Women want what they can't have: for men to be like them. From a male perspective, this is a very tall order. Men are very similar to women in many ways. Both are human. Both come from a mother and father. Both are social creatures. According to Abraham Maslow, the famous psychology professor who created Maslow's hierarchy of needs, all humans require the physical necessities of life; food, clothing and shelter to survive. Perhaps it is where physical needs end and esteem needs begin in Maslow's Hierarchy of Needs where men and women truly begin to differ.

Every human being has a unique personality. Every person has their own style. Take into account gender differences and the complexities for uniqueness expand even further.

Have you ever wished for someone, male or female, who could truly understand you? At some point we all say to ourselves, "gee, I wish there was someone on the face of this earth more like me or someone who knew where I was coming from." Most people need to feel understood and accepted. Relationships are no different. People get into relationships to love and be loved and also find someone who will validate their behaviors, thoughts, and dreams. This is the tricky part of relationships because this is where gender differences pose problems. Furthermore, women notice how great these differences really are once they get to know their mates.

By socialization, women are the more nurturing of the two sexes. To be nurturing is to be patient and empathetic. Whether consciously or unconsciously, women are in the driver's seat of intimacy and they need to teach men how to express their feelings.

Women, looking for their prize male, may not be able to catch him or reel him in! When another male comes along, a little less desirable, but workable, she may believe he can be molded into someone a little more desirable. She has her work cut out for her and will have to invest time, energy, and affection to change her man.

Of course the foregoing does not apply to all women, but it does happen for a large majority. These women want what they can't have! They want a man who behaves and thinks like them! They want a "best friend" who they can share their deepest, darkest secrets with and not be judged. Most want someone like their female best friend who they can trust and go to when they need to talk. They want a man who can be more like themselves; spontaneous, open-minded, not a control freak and one who is not egotistically challenged.

Most importantly women want men who are able to adapt and change as people and situations evolve. Sigmund Freud often used the term fixated to refer to individuals who were trapped in certain frames of their lives and unable to move onward. Freud believed one becomes fixated on parts of their lives where everything feels safe and secure with the chance of very little threat. Many women would assert that men become fixated on their pasts and become too comfortable with relationships and themselves. Being comfortable with others and one selves is good, but some women denote "comfort" with "taking for granted." Many men are guilty of this.

Change poses disruption to the smooth sailing waters in a man's life. Why rock the boat? Men would like to keep things as they are and are quite content to become fixated on a statuesque relationship. Women want more. They want a man who is willing to evolve in a relationship as they continue to grow. This is what women really want!

CASE STUDY

Jane is so tired and fed up with being misunderstood by men. The last three relationships she has had started out really well and it seemed her and each of her mates had so much to talk about each time. As the relationships progressed, it seemed to her the men she chose became less tolerant of her requests to communicate at deeper intimate levels. In fact, the more she tried to get them to open up, it seemed the more they tended to raise their voices and almost yell at her. She wasn't deaf! Also, she was not implying they were hard of hearing. It seemed they just weren't listening to what she was saying. When she asked them about their "future" together, they would respond about "living one day at a time" and "no rush to jump into anything too serious." This confused her greatly because in the beginning, it was they who had pursued her and literally begged her to marry them. Now that they knew they had her affection, the tables had turned. Was Jane really expecting too much of her mates? Had her mates deceived her into making her believe they were something they really weren't? Are they able and willing to understand her point of view and where she is coming from? How can they start out being so emotionally hot only to have their communicative emotions dwindle to a flicker? Finally, what also caught Jane's attention, was the fact that when she had enough and was ready to bail from the relationship, her mates would come on emotionally strong and "promise" to love her more and of course "change." They would be the type of communicator Jane wanted them to be! Well, do you think this change is possible after the many years of who and what they are? Should Jane wait or hope for them to change into what she wants them to be? If they change for Jane, is it because they really love her, or is it more out of fear of losing what they want?

• Women want men to be more like them...expressive, intimate communicators. What would you do if you were Jane?

CHAPTER THREE

WOMEN WANT WHAT THEY CAN'T HAVE: FOR MEN TO CHANGE... AND WHEN THEY DON'T THEY PUNISH THEMSELVES!

Women want mediocre men, and men are working hard to become as mediocre as possible.

Margaret Mead

To behave and think more like a woman means a man is going to have to change. What does change mean? Change means love! Changing for the purpose of improving a relationship shows your love for someone. He must first change for himself because he wants to change. Often times I hear men say they promise to change or will change for their mate. Wrong! This is not what women want. Rather they want a man to change for himself and in doing so he proves he really loves himself and his spouse.

How many times have you been told by your mate they would change to make you happy? What does this change mean? To put it bluntly, it means they will change to "shut you up" or get you off their back! They are contemplating change for the wrong reasons. Furthermore, they aren't really contemplating change because they believe it is needed, rather they

do so to avoid some sort of "punishment" which might include; "silent treatment", separation or divorce. In Behaviorism/Operant Conditioning, famous psychologist B.F. Skinner studied how rats avoid situations to avoid punishment and indulge in activities which bring rewards. Skinner's studies are very applicable to humans as they are the cornerstone for "timeouts" used in behavioral modification used with disruptive children. Humans modify existing negative behaviors to create a situation which maximizes rewards and minimizes punishment. Men who "change" for their wives often times do so for this same principle. The major criticism of Skinner and other behaviorists is that they assume people can't think for themselves, rather external influences cause them to modify existing behaviors. Therefore, there is little intrinsic value for men changing to appease their wives because it hasn't truly come from within. Interestingly, men who claim to change then go back to the way they were are often accused by women as being liars or "rats." Coercing someone into changing to make you happy is not going to work. It may last for a few weeks or a couple of months, but people are creatures of habit and will return to their old habits.

Women want what they can't have at the outset of a relationship: a man who thinks and acts like them. In the beginning, false pretenses may work! Many men will tell women what he thinks she wants to hear if it means he will have a chance in starting a relationship with her or just having sex with her. Men are very visual, physical, sexual creatures by their very nature and "adapt to survive", in this case survival connotes getting the woman!

IT'S LIKE HE CHANGED OVERNIGHT!

Many women who experience repeated failed relationships will often times say, "he was so nice and caring in the beginning, but as the relationship went on he changed and became someone I didn't even know." True and not true! The truth to this statement is most times we really do not truly know someone until we spend much time with them and see them in a multitude of situations involving a great number of different people. As far as the actual duration of time, you are probably looking at nine months to a year with the varying situations to really see a person's true colors. Even then, you may not see everything if the person wears a lot of masks and is really good at fooling others. I remember something a client once told me who was going through a divorce. He said, "tragic times reveal the true essence of a person and a bitter divorce reveals the true ugliness of your mate." His statement was very true. Even though we think we know someone, there is always the possibility for something to happen which brings out something in our mate we were never aware of.

I believe the statement to be true when we haven't spent enough time with our mates, or are just getting acquainted with them when we can honestly voice the statement, "I honestly didn't know them!" Most people in long-term relationships know their mates inside out but often times close a blind eye or turn a deaf ear. Once again there are those who are good at hiding their true selves, such as those with certain Personality Disorders as listed in the Diagnostic and Statistical Manual of Mental Disorders (DSM-IV), but they are few and far between.

In essence, most of the time you get what you get! Going back to the statement, "he was so nice in the beginning, but he seemed to change overnight" is a falsity and makes the statement untrue the majority of the time unless for the reasons I have otherwise stated. Most people know who and what they are getting when they meet someone. Furthermore, as the relationship progresses, you really know who and what you have. Women asserting, "he changed overnight, grew horns and donned a pitchfork" are trying to deny the fact they made a bad choice and now they have to wallow in their misery. If I sound cruel, then so be it, but you made a bad choice...deal with it! Men also make bad choices and they must also deal with them.

Women want what they can't have: a man who thinks and acts like them. In the beginning, some men pretend to think and act like them. The pretenses quickly fade as time passes. Most women are highly intuitive and intelligent enough to see through the facade. Many women see the deception but turn the other cheek. Are they blind? No. Are they stupid? No. Are they ignorant? No. Are they foolish? Yes! Women are foolish enough to believe their man will change for them, or believe they can change him.

I THOUGHT HE WOULD CHANGE!

As the relationship progressively gets worse, she keeps hoping for change but knows it will probably never happen. Why does she stay? I believe to protect her ego! Men are criticized for possessing big egos, but women have them too. Unfortunately, many women's egos gravitate around masochism. When I refer to masochism, I define it as having the following qualities: self-sacrificing, depressed, inhibited, fear of rejection and assuming oweness for lack of fruition in the relationship. In essence, she feels the need to punish herself for the bad choices she made. She chose someone who turned out to be a "bad" choice and now she chooses to punish herself for making the bad choice.

Perhaps the unconscious, irrational way for dealing with the situation is to turn it around. Rather than view him as a bad choice, she views him as "potential", a work in progress. "I didn't make a bad choice, rather he changed and now I have to 'unchange' him." Simply put, you stay in a bad relationship and hope he changes or you believe you can make him change.

UNDOING THE PAST

Do you have repeated failed relationships? In these failed relationships, is it the same type of guy each time that you attract? Does it seem each of these men are worse than the last? If so, you are probably a product of failed past relationships. We are all products of our pasts as our pasts shape us into who we are. Our pasts create us and give us our personalities and self-esteem albeit most of this is accomplished in middle to late childhood.

Our parents teach us what love is and what it is not. According to Hazan and Shaver (1987), their Attachment Theory of Love asserts that the quality of the attachment between the child and parent affects the child's ability to form romantic relationships when they are older. Furthermore, Hazan and Shaver (1987) claim three possible types of "lovers" are produced from the attachments between parents and children:

1) Secure Lovers · Those who don't fear abandonment because their parents always made them feel loved and accepted. Later in life, these individuals want to get close to others and do not fear abandonment and rejection.

2) Avoidant Lovers · Those with poor and weak attachments with their parents as children. These people are likely to have difficulty trusting partners and allowing others to get close to them.

3) Anxious-Ambivalent Lovers - Those with bad relationships who were rejected by their parents when they were children. These adults are likely to be overly dependent on others and try extra hard to get close to people. Unfortunately, they usually scare their partners off with their clinging behaviors.

According to the latter two types of Love, Hazan and Shaver (1987) assert that individuals coming from these type of backgrounds will have trouble forming and maintaining healthy types of relationships. These people are most likely to move from relationship to relationship never feeling fulfilled, or having relationships fail only to ask "why?"

Why do women keep attracting the same type of man? Perhaps to undo what was done in the past to them. Using the Hazan and Shaver's Attachment Theory, people are likely to revert back to what they are familiar and comfortable with. If you have had repeated failure and rejection in your life, you are probably familiar with the feelings even though you don't like them. No one wants to be rejected or made to fail, but when it happens enough times we begin to believe that is who we are. We think it, we feel it, with repetition we believe it, and finally we become it! If a woman attracts abusive or cold-hearted men, she might truly believe she deserves them because she is the same way.

In the world of psychology and social work, there is a term referred to as the "looking-glass self" (Cooley, 1922). This theory basically states that we see ourselves in those we associate with because they are very much like ourselves. "Birds of a feather flock together" is what it really asserts. We seek out people who are like us in behaviors and personality because we can relate to them and understand them. Also, when they accept our friendship and love, they validate who we are and most of the time condone our behaviors and beliefs. This is interesting when you apply it to women who experience abusive relationship after abusive relationship. Do these women seek out abusive or non-loving males because they themselves are that way?

Or, is it their vulnerability (low self-esteem) which makes them easy prey for men they would rather not date, but settle for because they feel they can get no better? Or is it just repeated chance and coincidence? Some women really believe they keep winding up with "winners" due to mere chance. Wrong!

Going back to the premise; you think, you feel, you believe, you become. Women who are repeatedly abused or those who experience repeated failure in relationships develop a self-esteem reflective of their past relationships. If you believe you are a failure, then you will start to act like a failure in the world of love and act in ways which reflect failure. How do you act in ways which reflect failure? Here is a five step process:

1) Give off vibes which denote low self-esteem. Your attitude and personality tell the world about you.

2) Looking-Glass Self - choose to associate with others who are like you. If you have low self-esteem, then you attract others or seek out others consciously or

subconsciously with low self-esteem.

3) Self-Fulfilling Prophecies - you set yourself up for failure. You actively choose men or situations which will affirm your inability to maintain or have a healthy relationship. When the relationship ends, you look in the mirror and tell yourself, "See, I told you so." This is achieving what you believe in. If you believe in failure, you'll get it!

4) Stereotyping/Attributing- taking one or more bad situations and extrapolating them to include the majority or all of the male population. Some women are so angry with men as a result of failed relationships, they walk around with negative attitudes toward all men. If you are overly critical of men, you are likely to chase the sensible ones away and wind up with critical males who have also been "burned" like yourself..."birds of a feather flock together" and "misery loves company."

5) Helplessness - believe you are helpless and hopeless. Someone above and beyond you has it in for you and that's just the way fate is. You have been dealt a terrible hand of cards and you just have to play them, and it will always be that way. After a while, you just give up and settle for whatever comes your way. Why? Because you believe you deserve no better and everything is just hopeless.

Everyone is a product of their past. Everyone who is alive is also in control of their present moment. If you are reading this right now, then you are in your present state of mind. You can choose to read this or put this down because you are in control. The same is true about relationships. Most of us consciously or unconsciously choose to hold on to the past because it represents familiarity and comfort. If women choose the same types of men repeatedly because they are similar to whom they've had in the past, then are men also not as likely to choose women who remind them of women from their own past relationships? Probably! If so, what does this mean? You have two people who will keep entering relationships with unresolved issues from previous relationships. Men are also products of their pasts but less likely to change. Why? If they don't perceive themselves as broken, then they won't fix it. Men are less likely to admit to and realize they have unresolved issues, and believe they are not the problem. Rather, they are more likely to believe it was the woman who was the problem. Women may take their unresolved issues into a relationship, but because they are less threatened by change, they are more likely to monitor issues as they arise.

Men will assert, "I'm the same guy today that I was ten years ago! I haven't changed!" Indeed, he probably hasn't. He has already admitted to you he hasn't changed. Do you really think he is going to change for you? Do you think you can change him? Are you ready to flog a dead horse?

Women want what they can't have: for men to evolve with them! Most men want what they already have: to remain the same! In the chapters to follow, you will see why men refuse to change.

CASE STUDY

Rikki was raised in a pretty decent family. She had two younger brothers, her mother worked full-time as a waitress and her father worked seven days a week in a factory. Her father was a good provider and saw to it that the family had everything it needed, i.e., food, clothes, shelter, etc. Her father seemed to show favoritism to her two younger brothers. As far back as she could remember, her father always took her brothers to their sporting events and always had time for them. He never made any time for her. In fact, by the age of eight, she began doubting that her father ever loved her. Now, at the age of 33, Rikki still longs to have a loving relationship with her father. However, her father still seems unable to love her the way she wants to be loved. Rikki has been married twice already and is living in a common-law marriage with her new partner. She loves her new partner very much, but they spend very little time with one another. He is always away on business. Her two previous husbands were also very hard workers who also engrossed themselves into their work. After some short-term counseling, Rikki's counselor posed an interesting question to her. She asked her if she was really "in love" with her current mate, or was she in love with the idea of "being in love." After discussing this with Rikki, Rikki concluded she was "in love" with the idea of a man loving her unconditionally. In fact, she wanted a man like her father who she could make love her the way her father never did. Rikki had chosen psychological representations of her father to compensate for the rejection she experienced as a young child. It was her goal to undo her father's emotional neglect toward her by making another man accept her. Interestingly, when the counselor asked her if she would love the man even more after she "made" him love her unconditionally, she replied by saying she never really thought that far ahead.

■ Is it better to be with someone for all the wrong reasons because you are afraid or uncomfortable being alone, or is it better to be single for the right reasons until you get your affairs in order?

CHAPTER FOUR

WOMEN WANT MEN TO EVOLVE

If a relationship is to evolve, it must go through a series of endings.

Lisa Moriyama

Growth is a very vague term. When most of us examine this term on the surface level, we are most likely to form some physical perception of something growing before our eyes. When we were children, we were taught to sow seeds and water them and make sure they got plenty of sunlight so they would grow and produce flowers. Because of our toiling, we were able to watch our hard work pay off and see a beautiful plant grow. Most of us kept this perception of "growth" in our minds to connote some physical change which we could visually measure.

Men tend to be more visual by nature. I will spend more time discussing this in a later chapter. Since they tend to be more visual, they are likely to measure change according to physical growth or something they can measure. Men prefer the tangibles!

People communicate primarily two different ways: verbally and non-verbally. The majority of our communication is in the non-verbal realm. When we converse verbally, most of our verbal words often carry strong non-verbal messages. Also, these verbal and non-verbal messages are analyzed and interpreted to mean several things by the trained listener. Every word spoken has two meanings: a denotative meaning and a connotative meaning.

Denotative meanings say what they mean. For example, when you say the word "cat" you mean the word cat; a four-legged, fluffy, little domestic pet. Connotative meanings, on the other hand, are the implied, underlying, emotional overtones which encompass a spoken word. For example, when one says the word "cat" it could connotatively be construed to mean a host of things: independent and cold, calculating and cruel, smooth and graceful, etc. What does this have to do with men, women, growth and relationships?

Women tend to communicate at the connotative level. Men tend to stay in the denotative domain. A woman says to her man, "you're a dog," he responds, "yeah, whatever." A man says to his woman, "you're a fox," she responds, "what do you mean by that, sexy or sarcastically sexist?"

Most men are likely to accept words spoken at face value. On the other hand, most women are likely to look deep within the spoken word to figure out what context the word was meant to imply. A word only means what the person speaking it was intending it to mean! People give words meanings, feelings and experiences. Women are trained listeners and know what to listen for in spoken words. They tend to be more analytical over the fewest of words spoken. Men, on the other hand, can take an essay and derive one simple meaning from it; exactly what it said!

Women look for the deepest of meanings in spoken words. Men look for the simplest meaning of the spoken word. The less emotion connoting the word, the better. Accept things for what they are. "Growth" is one of these words containing a very loaded connotative meaning. In fact, the word "growth" is a very trite term. Already, you can see the word "growth" can mean so many different things metaphorically, but when you toss in differences in gender perceptions you have created an amazing gap in communication.

Most men are likely to view growth from the frame of reference similar to the "plant growth" example I offered. Since men are more denotative in their communication skills, they are more likely to look for the tangible; something they can see and measure. They are more visual and they need to see it to believe and understand. Women, on the other hand, are more connotative and look for the intangibles. Just seeing the plant grow is not enough for them, rather the entire process is what is most fulfilling.

Men finish a project and see the finished product and are satisfied with the end result. They know what the sum of the parts were which created the whole finished product. Women look at the sum of the parts of the whole and see how everything is pieced together but then ask "why?" Have you ever asked your husband a question about something he built and he responds with something like, "it's just the way it is and that's that." You ask him, "but why?" and he responds with the same answer, "because it is the way it is, why does there have to be anything else?"

As long as he can see it, that's enough for him. As long as you can see it, then it's going to stimulate you to think and ask questions. He is content with the cause-effect outcome, while you are concerned about all the gaps which fill in the cause-effect process.

When he hears the word "growth", he pictures a blueprint, the steps involved, and the end product. When you hear the word "growth" you are also likely to see blueprints and end-products but also intangible components most men are likely to be naive to perceive. What are these intangible components?

They are the emotional, psychological, and social units comprised within any "growth" process for life. Using something very basic like a carpentry project, for example, I am sure you have seen the emotional, psychological and social components in action. I realize this is a very simple example, but I am sure you can relate. Your husband assembles something and you offer to help, but he says "no, I can do it myself." He struggles to put whatever it is together. Actually, it takes him two or three times longer than it should. You read the blueprint aloud and offer some advice and this really annoys him. He swears, curses and even throws things. The project becomes a thorn in his side. He is going to get the "damn thing" put together even if it kills

him! After a while, you have to leave the room because his cursing is giving you a headache and you seem to be a catalyst for his building rage. Hours later he appears and grabs your hand. He has a big smile on his face. He has "something to show you!" He leads you to the finished project and proudly displays his masterpiece. At this point you probably care less about his "amazing feat" and are content to just nod your head. Finishing something is what was important to him. Furthermore, the challenge of succeeding on his own was even more important. This is how women and men view change differently. Men look for the tangibles while women look for the intangibles. Their perceptions on change closely resemble the do-it-yourself project.

Women want men to grow. Growth means change. For men, growth means seeing something tangible, i.e., an end product, which they can measure immediately by its completion. Second, men who grow and change want to do it by themselves and do not want women to help them. Let's examine the tangible change first.

Let's use the example of a dysfunctional relationship where the wife experiences physical abuse. The couple has been together for 4 years, one year dating and three years married. During the dating year, the husband was verbally aggressive at times, but never hit her. When she began worrying her mate's verbal aggression might escalate into physical violence and confronted him, he assured her it wouldn't. In fact, the reason he got so upset with her was he "loved her so much and just hated being away from her". Even though she didn't like the way he spoke to her, yelled at her, and called her names, the promises, melodramatic apologies, and flowers he gave to her always brought some silver lining to the black clouds. Most importantly, he said things would change once they were married and in some ways she was flattered by the attention he showed her. Remember, he acted the way he did because he "loved her and couldn't stand to be away from her." Sound familiar?

Once into the marriage, the verbal abuse progressed into physical assault. Each time he hit her or beat her she would threaten to leave him but he would apologize. He would also promise to change. In his mind he did change. Instead of beating her once a week, it was every two or three weeks. When he did strike her, he would say, "see, I'm trying hard to change...I went three weeks without blowing up or hitting you." What is he really saying to himself? "It's your fault I hit you and I was doing damn good...I should get the apology from you for having had to hit you!" The scary part is, many women who are in abusive relationships really believe it is their fault. He uses the tangible change, not hitting her in three weeks, to justify his "growth" process. He really truly believes he has done well based on the completed project, three weeks without beating her. Unfortunately, just as his thinking is irrational, so is her own for condoning his concept of change.

A less complex, more simple example is where the wife wants her husband to be more romantic and show more public displays of affection. To stop her "nagging" he promises to change and try harder. For the next month, whenever they are out in public he makes the extra effort to hold her hand. He even keeps score of how many times he has done so. When she questions his love and affection for her months later, after he has slacked off in is affectionate displays, he has a running scorecard of times he has held her hand to read in his defense. This only makes her more upset and hurt. Why? Tangible change! Women are aware of tangible change and see it as something quantifiable, like notches in a gunfighter's gun belt. She knows the record he keeps is nothing more than a running scorecard to throw in her face at a later date. If he was sincere in his heart at changing, he would not have to keep track of being affectionate. Men keep track of things such as "favors" because they are taught early in life what it means to "owe" someone something. Men are taught about "one-up-man-ship", which means someone owes them a favor or they owe someone a favor. Many men are taught that to owe someone is a sign of weakness or failure. Therefore, most men would rather sink than owe someone else, especially a woman, a favor. Why do you think men are reluctant to stop and ask for directions when they are lost? Because they might owe someone something later on or show they are a failure at finding their destination!

Men who keep a running record of their "changes" in essence are telling women "you owe me, back off!" In their minds they really believe they have made sacrifices by trying to change and when they fall back into their old ways, women should back off and stay quiet. They believe they have done enough and women owe them a debt of gratitude and can begin to repay them by keeping their mouths shut!

The second part of the growth process in males comes in the form of independence and mastery. If and when confronted with the challenge of having to change, they are going to do it alone. If their wife or girlfriend tells them they need to change, they will usually respond in one of two ways. First, they will disregard their mate's request for change and fight them all the more. If they don't fight you, then the second response to change will occur. He will make a solo attempt at changing himself and all bets are off when you try to interfere. "I'm trying to be what you want me to be, so back off!"

In one-up-man-ship, having character flaws or short-comings pointed out connotes weakness. If you point out flaws in his behaviors then his ego kicks in and he perceives your criticisms as being directed at his entire being. You criticize a specific behavior such as his not taking out the garbage and he perceives this as you calling him "lazy" or "useless." Most people are not able to separate one's personality from the behaviors they engage in. Since most people are not able to do this, the majority of people have a difficult time accepting constructive criticism. You have to separate the person from the behavior! Men are more likely to perceive constructive criticisms from women as jabs at their manhood, which in turn are further perceived as someone calling them weak. What do you do when someone calls you weak or inadequate? You fight them! You tell him to take out the garbage and he tells you "go to hell" and he lets the garbage pile up. He sees you get frustrated and angry and storm out of the house with the garbage bag. As soon as you leave, a glorious smile fills his face. In his mind he has won. No one, especially his wife is going to tell him what to do or how to do it!

The sarcastic quality of adult relationships is they become refurbished in child-like behaviors and mannerisms during conflicts. Children get into arguments and fights with the intention of winning. Adults are no different. Men are more competitive by nature and when you tell him to do something he will fight you.

He is not going to let you get one-up on him. He is not going to let you think you won. The more you ask him to change or try to change him, the more likely he is going to engage in the behavior you desire him to change to prove a point!

So he doesn't fight you and is man enough to accept your constructive criticism and admits to needing to change and grow. Then what? He is going to do it by himself! You offer to help or support him in his "changing." He won't accept your help for the simple reason he doesn't believe he needs help fixing a problem he doesn't have. You have created this problem for him and if it means working it out to quiet you then that is what he will do.

Whenever you comment on his lack of change the running scorecard is tossed in your face. He blames you for his lack for positive growth because you keeps criticizing him, nagging him, and preventing him from achieving the ultimate change you desire in him. You are damned if you do, damned if you don't!

Interestingly, when men feel they are about to lose their mate, they will readily admit of their own accord they have a problem and they will do whatever it needs to be fixed. When women come to their mates first and suggest something like counseling to repair or improve the relationship, men will refuse to see a "shrink." They often times assert, "there's nothing wrong with me or our relationship and we don't need some shrink to mess in our lives." Conversely, when she calls it quits, he is quick to lobby for the "shrink" to save the relationship. At this point it's too late. The proverbial "Elvis" has left the building and there is no getting him back!

To recap this chapter, women perceive change and growth in a connotative light. They see change as the opportunity to foster new personal growth. They are able to perceive the entire growth process in its entirety. Men, on the other hand, perceive change as a denotative experience. Many are only willing to see the start of the process and the end product. For them, the end outweighs the steps involved.

Women are more receptive to change and are likely to assist those who want to change. Men are more fixated on the present and all the past experiences which made them who they are today. Change threatens their core identity and many are resistant to change. Furthermore, when a woman suggests for her man to change or offers to help him change for the better he is likely to feel insulted and to fight her.

Women want men to evolve, but men are content to stay the way they are. Growth means change, and change represents the unknown which can be frightening to the male ego. If change is needed, then he must have some short-coming and this would mean she is stronger than him because she pointed it out. So he thinks!

CASE STUDY

Doug was referred to an anger management support group after his wife charged him with physical abuse. When his court date came up, his wife who had forgiven him tried to have the charges dropped, but the police charged him. Doug was granted leniency by the judge and ordered to take anger management counseling. At the first meeting, Doug claimed he didn't have any anger problems, but rather it was his wife's nagging and prodding which led him to hit her. In fact, his wife believed she was the main reason Doug hit her. If she just wouldn't have asked him so many "pointless" questions and continually nagged him about why he was late all the time, then he wouldn't have had to hit her. It was only the first time he had ever hit her! Up until that point he had shoved her on occasion and usually just swore at her. Each time he did warn her to "shut up" and stop nagging him.

Doug was doing quite well in the group over the first five weeks. He had no blow-ups at home until one night when he had too much to drink and his wife suggested he had had enough. Doug responded by hitting her, but this time she did not call the police. The next day while Doug was at work, she packed her things and left him. He found her at her sister's house. He was forbidden to set foot in the house. Doug began pleading and crying for her to come back. He swears it will not happen again. He claimed he had been "cured" for five weeks and it was her "nagging" which caused him to have the problem. He said he would continue going to the anger management group and get extra counseling to "get her back" and prove to her how much he loves her. His wife suggested he get the help and told him she was making no promises but will see how well he does.

- Is Doug changing for himself because he really believes he has a problem? Or is Doug changing to protect against his ego which he believes has been threatened by his wife leaving?

CHAPTER FIVE

SOCIETY HASN'T TRAINED MEN TO BE LIKE WOMEN

Saying that men talk about baseball in order to avoid talking about their feelings is the same as saying that women talk about their feelings in order to avoid talking about baseball.

Deborah Tannen, You Just Don't Understand

How many times have you heard someone or yourself say, "men, can't live with them, can't live without them"? How many of you have actually said it and really meant it? I'm sure many of you have. For the record, there are many men saying the same thing about women!

Women assert about men, "if they could only think more like us, then everything would be great." Most women love the company of a "good" man. Most women enjoy the physical intimacy of a man. Most women dream about getting married and having a family. Furthermore, most women dream about being with a man who can be more like them and understand them. This last wish is perhaps the tallest of orders!

Women want a man who will understand them better and be more like them. Most men are incapable of fulfilling this wish because they lack the proper skills. I'm sure many of you have heard about or read John Gray's, Men Are from Mars, Women Are from Venus self-help book. Gray does an excellent job of contrasting the differences which exist between men and women as if they were from two distinct planets. Gray is not too far off in his metaphorical premise. There are definite differences which exist between men and women. And for those who are studying current societal trends and relationships, you now have to consider not only heterosexual men and women but homosexual men and women. And you thought the differences were great between heterosexual men and women?

Why do men lack the communicative and emotional skills women seek? Are they really from a different planet? No, even though some women would vehemently contend they are no matter what proof you offer them! Men differ from women in their communicative skills and abilities because society has trained them differently. Men are less likely to express emotions and delve into the emotional intimacy world women master. Why? They don't know how!

I asserted earlier that men prefer to be in control and participate in experiences and events they know they are competent in or will succeed at. When you put most men into the world of emotional intimacy they are like fish out of water. Many lack the competence to express themselves and most realize it. Have you ever noticed when you try to get your mate to open up to you and express his emotions, it is like pulling teeth? Well, for many men they probably would rather be sitting in the dentist chair because they know the experience will come to an end no matter how painful it will be. Men do not know what they will get or where things will go when they express their deepest emotions to a woman. When a woman asks him to open up she is asking him to shed his egotistical, masculine persona and bare his vulnerable soul. This is extremely hard for him to do.

Women are much better at revealing their true feelings. Most are usually not afraid to express themselves in public. If they are happy they will publicly exude their joy. If they are sad they will show their grief and cry. Most men will display the same facial expressions for both happiness and sadness. Sometimes, the most a woman ever sees her man express himself is on Super Bowl Sunday!

Why do men find it so hard expressing their true feelings to women? Society has taught them to be the "strong, silent type." Interestingly, in the past, society also taught women the best catches were the strong and silent types.

When women married these men they found out that emotional intimacy didn't exist and society was wrong. Today, women prefer sensitive, expressive men. However, society hasn't yet caught up with female expectations.

Early in life, society trains men to be different from women. The obvious differences in gender anatomy are further broadened by psychological, mental, and emotional conditioning. It is for this very reason many men are intimately challenged!

INFANCY TO FIVE YEARS OF AGE

Most infants are born on an even playing field, regardless of their gender, over the first three years of life. No matter what socio-economic status the infant is raised in, gender qualities are not too pronounced at that point. Parents may dress girls in pink and boys in blue, which is fine. The color scheme does nothing more than identify the child by its specific gender. A little boy may know they are a "boy" just as a little girl may know they are a "girl", but as far as behavioral roles, both are still ignorant as to what is expected of them.

Many psychologists believe during the first two years of the child's life, it is very important for them to get lots of love and affection from their mothers. The best ways love will be shown in the first two years is through cuddling, holding, touching and care-giving behaviors. Regardless of gender, the child learns love and affection through receiving it. Babies who are given lots of love and affection will grow into loving and affectionate little boys and girls.

Many children really don't start to bond with their fathers until around the ages of two to four. Many fathers, who take an active part in their children's lives are still learning the ropes about being a father. Many fathers treat their babies as very fragile creatures and usually consult with "mom" before doing anything too innovative or new with the child. Once the child becomes older and mom starts to teach dad he can play and do more things with his child, his influence becomes more predominant, especially for little boys. It is around four years of age when dad becomes a stronger influence in his child's life.

Many children become interested in their bodies around two to three years of age. They begin noticing and showing interest in their genitals. Studies have shown that sexually inquisitive behaviors reach a peak in children in the three to five year age period (Friedrich et al., 1991). Boys and girls play games and undress where they show their bodies and genitals to one another. Many children play doctor at this age and it really upsets and worries parents. These sexually explorative games are healthy and harmless child behaviors.

Some boys and girls question their sexuality during this age period. It is during this age period where some little girls wished they were boys and had a penis. Some girls actually mimic or try to copy boys by trying to stand up while urinating. Some boys, on the other hand, wish they could be more like girls and play games like dress-up, house, and skip-rope. Most mothers do not feel threatened by their children's behaviors and find them rather cute and charming. Some mothers take pictures of their five year old sons wearing a dress, make-up, and a wig while playing house. Fathers, on the other hand, are very worried by this behavior and quickly try to remedy the situation. They perceive this as a problem and their homophobic worries kick into over-drive. It is at this point where they truly intervene in their sons' and daughters' lives.

They will not tolerate their sons dressing up like girls or playing girlish games. They will not tolerate their daughters playing doctor or house with little boys. Remember, men are thinking like men and not children! Interestingly, if their daughters choose to participate in sports, fathers are usually the first to encourage it and find it "cute" that their daughter wants to be a hockey player. Mothers don't get too upset with this, however. Why? Gender differences in their perceptions of rearing children, which were created in childhood. It is a cycle which continues when fathers are added into the gender socializing formula. When fathers intervene and disallow their sons from playing girlish games, they are setting the socialization process in motion. Society has taught fathers that boys are strong, less sensitive, and more masculine than girls. Girls are weak, fragile, emotional, feminine creatures needing protection. Therefore, boys are not allowed to play house, dress-up, or skip-rope because fathers believe it will impede their masculine growth. Many fathers enroll their sons in masculine activities such as team sports, promoting rough and tumble behaviors.

AGE SIX ONWARD

Fathers have intervened in their son's lives for better or for worse. Regardless of whether a child comes from a traditional family home or a single parent home, as long as the father is present, some of the time he will have a masculinizing effect on his son's life. Fathers are role models for both male and female children. In fact, fathers may be even more important than mothers in teaching children respect for the opposite sex when older. By watching his father interact with his mother, a son learns how men are to treat women. By watching her father interact with her mother, a daughter learns how women are to be treated by men. Since daughters spend more time being socialized by their mothers and other women, they pretty much stay on the social learning track they were on since infancy. Boys, on the other hand, are plucked away from the earlier socialization process and strewn into one which is laden with male dominance and expectation.

The social learning path girls stay on, and the one boys were once on, is not totally or purely feminine. If males were more open-minded to the socialization process, which they aren't because of the reasons I just explained, they would realize the path converges into an androgynous intersection.

Androgyny is the ability to play both male and female roles where appropriate. A male can play a more masculine role while playing a game of pick-up hockey with the guys. On the other hand, the same male can play a more feminine, nurturing role with his one year old son when he needs to be bottle-fed.

Women play the androgynous role better than men. The famous psychiatrist, Carl G. Jung, referred to the evolution of androgyny later in life for adults when they retire and move into their senior years. Women, whose children have grown and left home, are now free to do more activities outside of the home. They relinquish their duties as primary caregivers and seek out more assertive activities. Men, who are now at retirement age or retired, lose their "career" identity and no longer are required to play the role of breadwinner. Instead of working, they begin to spend more quality time with their grandchildren and become more nurturing. Jung believed this shift occurs for most adults later in life. Jung made this assertion long before women's rights movements, equality in the workplace, women going to colleges and universities, and the single parent household. I am sure many sociologists and psychologists who subscribe to Jung's theory would hold to it that women are becoming more assertive earlier on in life because of single-parenthood and their desire to establish successful careers. The same can be said about single fathers raising their children who, too, are pressed into more nurturing roles.

Women have always played the androgynous role. They have been taught to from the time they were old enough to grasp it. Boys wanted to learn the role but got their wings snipped by their fathers before they could take flight. Even though boys were taken away from many of the activities girls do, most girls were not forced away from the many activities boys do. In fact, today young girls are encouraged to take up many of the sporting activities boys have traditionally excelled in.

Young girls are allowed to participate in traditional girlish activities and boyish activities. Boys on the other hand are removed from girlish activities and segregated into the male world of sports. Does this really have an impact? Some would assert it's just fun and games boys are being mainstreamed into. Well, I think there are more than just "games" to consider here.

When boys are prevented from playing with girls, they are also denied the chance to better understand girls. They are prevented from learning the same kinds of communication skills girls have the chance to learn. Boys are thrown into an "all male mix" void of communication skills which will eventually flourish into intimacy mastery.

Because boys are taken away from the female world early on in life, they are unable to be like women in their communication abilities. This quality is further compounded by the fact that most girls are still allowed to participate in boyish activities as well as their own. What happens is that the females get the jump on in their abilities to better understand males. They watch, observe, and literally understand what makes a male tick: ego and pride!

Androgyny is a very important quality females learn and possess early on in life. Boys were just getting around to developing it before they were so rudely plucked away by their fathers. To be androgynous is to see both sides of the coin. Girls have this ability because they were allowed to flourish socially without much disruption. Women want men to be more like them but they can't. They just don't know how! Unfortunately, boys were robbed by their fathers and just not given the time to develop.

CASE STUDY

Trevor was often picked on as a child. When he was in elementary school, he often used to play skip rope, four square, and other games with the girls. At home, he used to spend a lot of time with his older sister and single mother. His father would occasionally come by and take him out. He despised his father and the way he abused his mother. At school, Trevor was often picked on by the other boys because he played with the girls. They used to refer to Trevor as a "prissy" and "sissy." Whenever Trevor played sports in gym class, the boys used to pick on him. When Trevor entered high school, he noticed the boys picked on him less and he continued to meet new girls and spend time with them. By senior year Trevor had dated several girls, never really being too serious with any of them. Most of the girls continued to be close friends after they stopped dating as they felt they could connect with him at an emotional level and he understood them. In fact, some of the guys from his elementary school years would now come to him for advice on how to speak to girls or make things right in their own relationships. The boys no longer referred to Trevor as a "queer." As a matter of fact, Trevor received the affectionate name "lady killer" from the guys. Trevor finally settled down when he was 29 and married a woman he met while he was vacationing in Europe. The two have been happily married for 7 years and they have two children. Trevor works part-time on his career as a music composer so he can stay at home and raise his boys while he encouraged his wife to pursue her career as an attorney. Trevor was able to apply all the rules on how to treat others the way his mother treated him and how not to treat others as he learned from his father. Trevor did not turn out "gay" as some theorists would believe would be the case and he did not turn out a loner. On the contrary, he grew into an emotionally strong, androgynous man.

■ Do you believe the stereotype that men who are in touch with their feelings and not afraid to express their emotions are still viewed as "weak" by men in today's society?

CHAPTER SIX

MEN CAN'T BE LIKE WOMEN BECAUSE THEY HAVEN'T OBSERVED MEN BEHAVING AS WOMEN DO IN THEIR OWN LIVES

All women become like their mothers. That is their tragedy. No man does. That is his.

Oscar Wilde

Men can't be like women because they haven't observed men behaving as women do in their own lives! As mentioned in the last chapter, the most time males and females spend together on an equal playing field for communication is up until the age of five or six. After this age, fathers remove their sons away from primary female influence and socialize them into the masculine beings they become.

It is not until adolescence when males and females begin to spend more time together. By this point, socialization differences are defined enough to separate masculinity from femininity. Males fight any and all insinuations that might be feminine, let alone androgynous! It is during this period of their lives that males try extra hard to be masculine. The onset of puberty definitely reinforces this process.

People are by-products of their environments. To be more accurate, children learn from observing and interacting with their parents. Psychologist Albert Bandura, who coined the social learning theory, asserted that we are created by who is around us. The social learning theory states that individuals become who they are from observing those closest to them, whom they perceive as role models. By observing those closest to them, children begin to model themselves and act in ways similar to their mentors. Who is a child's mentor? Typically their parents.

As I mentioned earlier, most children begin to be strongly influenced into gender socialization after five years of age. Children become more aware of the world around them and the roles they are to play. Most children begin to develop gender schemas, (Bem, 1983), which are mentally organized patterns of behavior that help children sort out the information they receive in their lives. Children begin to develop a true concept of what it is to be male or female. Children then adapt their own sets of behaviors and attitudes about what boys and girls are supposed to do. They learn gender appropriate behaviors for the gender roles they are expected to possess.

❋ Psychoanalytic theory asserts that children develop their gender roles as a function of their sexual focus and the attachments they have to their parents.

❋ Freud believed children act the way they do and become what they are because they go through a psychosexual stage in their lives referred to as the Phallic stage. In this stage, children become biologically gratified by focusing on their genitals. Children touch themselves and explore their sexuality. Also, children begin to ask questions regarding their own sexuality.

In the Phallic stage, Freud also believed the psyche of the child develops its gender identity, and that children developed their sense of gender through their attachment with their parents. Furthermore, Freud believed children experience common anxieties and fears during this stage. While going through this stage, children experience one of two complexes. Boys experience what Freud called the Oedipus complex and girls the Electra complex.

The Oedipus complex boys experience is based on an ancient Greek Myth. In the myth, Oedipus kills his father and marries his mother. A boy develops a sexual attachment to his mother and views his father as the rival. The son views his father as the competitor who wants to take away his mother's love. Unconsciously, the son would like to see his father go away so he could take his place and be alone with his mom. The boy experiences an inner conflict between hostility for the father as well as affection for him. Finally, at some point when the boy notices that little girls don't have a penis, he wonders why. Moreover, his wondering leads to castration anxiety, where he worries that if his father finds out about his bad thoughts about him, he will castrate him. To stop the frightening thoughts and feelings, the boy represses his sexual desires for his mom and begins to over-identify with his father whom he perceives as the aggressor. From this point on, the son wants to be like dad and does whatever he can do to dispel any identification with his mother or femininity.

According to Freud, girls go through a similar identification process which he called the Electra complex. This, too, is based on a Greek story where the king's daughter, Electra, helps her brother murder their mother to avenge their father's death. According to Freud, the young girl develops a sexual attraction to the father and views her mother as her rival. Girls develop this complex because of penis envy. Penis envy occurs when girls begin to notice they don't have a penis, rather a small clitoris. They want a penis and many of them wish they could be little boys. Little girls believed they once had a penis but it was castrated and they in turn blame their mothers for letting this happen. To compensate for the lack of a penis, girls then develop a desire for motherhood. The only way she can achieve this is to marry her father and hope that her mother will go away. She tries to get closer to her father and replace her mother. When she realizes she cannot win, she gives up and turns to her mother and identifies with her as to covet a relationship with her father. Girls begin to identify with their mothers to learn and develop the feminine skills which will one day help them get a husband for themselves.

Even though Freud's theories were often times labeled absurd for the over-emphasis on sex, many are still used today as the basis for understanding personality. Psychoanalytical theories and social learning theories are used to explain behaviors and understand why people are the way they are.

Society has not trained men to be what women want them to be. If we use either of the theories, you can see how individuals are most likely to identify with the parent of the same sex. Boys learn from their fathers how to be males and girls learn from their mothers how to be females. Since androgyny tends to be a quality more readily associated as a female quality, girls are one-up on boys in gender socialization.

Girls know how to behave and act like females. Girls are also taught how to act androgynous. They can empathize more with males than males can with females. Boys, however, are taught how to act like males and most have this perfected.

Society has always been "male dominated." Even though various women's movements have tried to change things, most women will still assert "it's a man's world." Since it is a man's world, the way people are socialized will pretty much continue the same route. Girls are still taught to be feminine and androgynous. Society is trying hard to create more sensitive, understanding, androgynous males, but it is not the American way. Feminist groups would assert that the American way for males is one of competition, aggression, and even violence. If you examine most violent crimes committed, they are usually males who perpetrate these crimes. Society asks "why?" Well, society has created and refined males in the prototypical "male" mold. It is difficult to undo what has taken thousands of years to achieve: the male ego.

When young boys are given the chance to observe and model themselves after a parent, most, if not all, are going to want to be like "dad." Fathers were once boys who were in turn raised to be prototypical males. Obviously, they spent more time identifying with their own fathers or other male role models.

Men who behave like women are perceived as "sissies." How often have you witnessed a man cry in public? Rarely. How often have you seen a woman cry in public? Probably more often. The same is true for communication. Boys are more likely to turn to their mothers if they need to talk about something emotional. Often times, if a son comes to his father with an emotional issue, the father will say, "go tell your mom, she's better with these types of things."

Do you know what the cowboy syndrome (Balswick & Peck, 1971) is? The cowboy syndrome describes men who are inexpressive, strong, silent, and closed. This male would never cry, feel sorry for himself, ask for help, or experience fear. The syndrome is patterned off the behaviors seen in old spaghetti westerns and cowboy movies. Many men want to be like Sylvester Stallone or Clint Eastwood. It's the American way! Boys are more comfortable behaving this way because it's the way dad taught them . Fathers tell their sons not to cry because it shows others you are weak. Many young boys are taught not to get angry or express themselves because it shows fear and weakness. What we end up with are closed, frightened, angry, hurt children who grow into inexpressive men who lack intimacy skills.

Have you noticed the number of violent incidents that are occurring in American schools? What happened in Jonesboro, Arkansas in 1998 and what recently happened in Littleton, Colorado are growing phenomena's affecting society. Why is this happening? Possibly the cowboy syndrome? Boys are not being taught to express themselves appropriately. The tensions and stress in their lives build until they can no longer be kept in check. How do they respond? In ways they have witnessed or seen other males respond: aggressively and violently!

Have you ever heard the saying, "if every country was run by a female president or leader there would never be war and bloodshed"? Do you believe this statement? I do! The reason there would probably never be a serious war is because women would empathize and communicate at deeper intimate levels and understand the true meaning of humanity.

Men need to experience the world as women do! By trying to experience the world from a woman's perspective, not only will they be better communicators, but they will also be better fathers. Children, regardless of gender, need love and affection from both parents. Mothers give tremendous amounts of love and affection to their children. A mother's love, however, is not enough! Children need the love of both parents. A minority of men communicate with children and show them the love and affection they need. The problem is, these men are not a majority. The vast majority of fathers are "weekend dads." Due to divorce, separation, or career, the most quality time fathers spend with their children is driving them to and from their new homes or to their sporting events. This is not enough time well spent!

I heard a statistic last year on the radio which stated the average time spent between parents and children daily in effective communication is roughly about four and one-half minutes. Four and one-half minutes! I would assume the four and one-half minutes is due to single-parenthood and the stress of trying to work two or more part-time jobs to satisfy financial burdens. Interestingly, the same statistic also asserted that the average time couples spend in effective and meaningful communication each day is roughly around twelve and one-half minutes. No wonder divorce and separation rates are so high!

The majority of men do not know how to communicate with their children because their fathers did not know how to communicate with them. This miscommunication cycle is passed on from generation to generation and rarely gets remedied or corrected. As stated in previous chapters, men are usually not likely to grow because it means change and these changes are threatening for they go against what they were taught early on in life.

Boys need to see men participating in more androgynous roles and doing the kinds of activities women do. Men need to be told by other men they mentor themselves after that it's okay to be androgynous. Most importantly, men have to create emotional identities they are most comfortable with rather than what society dictates. This, however, is easier said than done. Men need positive, communicative role models. There are not enough of them out there. There are Christian men's groups which have rallies across North America to work with men who are violent or have substance abuse problems. These same types of groups are needed to teach men it's okay to be human and be emotional creatures. Perhaps elementary and secondary schools need to create curriculums which teach students courses in life skills and what it is to be human. With the uprising of violence and divorce rates in our society, they are long overdue.

CASE STUDY

A fifteen year old adolescent named Craig describes what it is like to be a male in his household. He tells his story:

"In my house there is my mother, my older sister, younger brother and my father, who is hardly ever around. He is either working or out with his friends playing hockey. My father got my brother and I into hockey when we were younger, but I quit playing because my brother was a lot better at it than I was. My father had wanted to play professional hockey but didn't make it. He kind of wanted me to be the hockey player he wasn't. He used to coach my team. I was the captain. Whenever I had a bad game, my father would make me wear a dress when we got home for the rest of the night. He used to tell me if I played like a girl, I might as well dress like a girl. He no longer coaches hockey; many of the parents used to get mad at him and had him banned from coaching. He does go and watch my brother's games and yells at him, but not so much. My brother plays goalie and gets invited with the traveling team all the time. This makes my father proud of him. I feel like I am kind of forgotten. My mother spends a lot of time with my sister doing girl stuff and that bores the heck out of me. Last summer I met some new friends and we have started hanging out. This one guy has a gun and it is really neat. His father was in the army and has a gun collection in his basement. His father tells his son that he wants him to be in the army one day too. He wants to be so his father will be pleased. I wish my father was pleased with me. I just wanted him to like me more. What can I do to make him like me?"

• Craig lacks a true father figure in his life. Fathers need to love all of their children unconditionally and recognize them for who and what they are. Fathers are who their sons look up to the most!

CHAPTER SEVEN

MEN CAN'T BE LIKE WOMEN BECAUSE THEY DON'T WANT TO BE LIKE WOMEN FROM THEIR OWN EXPERIENCES

Women want mediocre men, and men are working hard to become as mediocre as possible.

Margaret Mead

Men can't be like women because they don't want to be like women from their own personal experiences. In the last chapter, I discussed how men have never observed men behaving as women do. The only people they are most likely to see behaving as women are women! There are some homophobic men who are highly critical of homosexual males who embellish feminine mannerisms, which perhaps further misconstrues the notion that it is bad to behave like a woman. Men do not want to be like women from their own experiences for three reasons: gender socialization, family socialization and personal experience.

GENDER SOCIALIZATION

What does society teach men about women? Do you think men perceive these qualities as positive?

Socialization is a process of internalizing societal beliefs. Whatever attitudes and behaviors are held acceptable in society at that particular moment in time are defined as the norm. Unfortunately, many norms are based on stereotypes, which are oversimplified, preconceived ideas that serve as short-cuts to perceptions. These oversimplified beliefs are applied to certain groups, such as minorities and genders.

Both, children and adults, often times base their perceptions of the opposite sex based on gender stereotypes. Many young children's ideas about their counterparts reflect over-simplified, concrete misrepresentations about "femininity" and "masculinity." Because most children think in concrete terms and some adults choose to, the way in which gender socialization is perceived is very one-dimensional and very polarized. Polarized thinking is the inability to perceive things abstractly and only in concrete terms. To be a polarized thinker is to think in "black and white" terms. Everything is seen at two ends of the continuum and there is no gray area.

Cognitive-behavioral psychiatrist, Aaron Beck, believes polarized thinking is a cognitive distortion which causes many individuals to think neurotically. When one thinks with polarized vision, they are unable to perceive the host of choices and possibilities which exist. As children, we are usually taught to think and perceive the world in "black/white" or "right/wrong" terms. The same holds true for gender socialization. Therefore, most children who are polarized thinkers only see things as either "masculine" or "feminine" with nothing, such as "androgyny" in between.

When children become teenagers are able to think in more logical terms, according to noted theorist, Jean Piaget, they are able to think more abstractly. To see more abstractly is to recognize middle terms like "androgyny." Since men are socialized into thinking in "masculine" ways, they refrain from changing because to change is a contradiction to "masculinity."

Therefore, men are more likely than females to remain polarized thinkers even though they have developed the abilities to think abstractly in their teens. Women tend to use their abstract, logical abilities to further refine their social skills, whereas most males use their abstract logical abilities to become better at "task oriented" projects. Recall a few chapters ago when we discussed how men are more concerned with getting the project done. This is an example of polarized thinking; one end of the continuum is "beginning" and the other end is "end."

How does society stereotypically socialize "masculinity" and "femininity?" Masculinity, by today's standards, is defined with the following qualities: dominant, assertive, aggressive, success and achievement oriented, highly competitive, very independent, strong, and emotionless. Femininity, by today's standards, is perceived as: very dependent, weak, docile, innocent, passive, co-operative, family-oriented, socially driven, and highly emotionally expressive.

If you were a male, which one of the two qualities would you perceive to be more positive? Femininity is stereotyped as the weaker of the two qualities, or that females are perceived by men as the weaker of the species. Why don't men want to be like females? They are perceived to be weak!

Studies by Lamb (1986) and Parke and O'Leary (1976) found that many fathers today use traditional stereotypical gender roles toward their infants. Fathers act as playmates to their infants, while mothers act as caregivers. To be a playmate is connoted differently from being a caregiver. A "caregiver" is nurturing and very feminine. A "playmate" is more rough and tumble and more masculine. Maybe you have heard this before: When a father watches over his children when his wife is away he is "stuck baby-sitting!" How can a parent "baby-sit" their own child? This is the way males are socialized in their paternal thinking schema.

Therefore, to be more feminine is to be perceived as weak and more subservient. Why don't men want to be more like women? Since men are more competitive than women, to be more like a woman is perceived as being "second best."

FAMILY SOCIALIZATION

Family is perhaps the best source of gender socialization for children. Traditionally, young children spend the majority of their time around parents and other family members. Lately, this has changed since children are spending more time in daycare centers, but the family is still the strongest influence on a child's gender perception.

Men observe their fathers and learn to become masculine by how their fathers behave. As early as infancy, fathers can have a profound effect on their son's perceptions about females and femininity. A study was done by Langlois and Downs in 1980. They observed young children playing with toys and how their mothers and fathers behaved around the children as they played. Boys and girls were both given toys to play with. The toys they were to play with were selected to match their gender. What they found was interesting. When fathers found their sons playing with "girl" toys, they reacted negatively and interfered with their son's playing. Mothers on the other hand, reacted the same way to both sons and daughters, regardless of whether they played with "girl" toys or "boy" toys. Mothers did not feel threatened in any way about their child's gender socialization.

Children mimic what they see. If boys are told "girl" toys are wrong, they are likely to unconsciously extrapolate these misconceptions about girls in general. They don't want to be like girls because girls are "bad" and "wrong." A girl gives a boy an innocent kiss on the cheek and he is quick to wipe it off. His friends chime in, "oooh, yuck, you're going to get cooties." Already, the lines are being drawn.

There are some fathers who will not change their infants diapers because they call it too "disgusting" and too "dirty." I'm sure many women feel that changing a diaper is disgusting and dirty at times, but they do it all the same. Fathers add to their gender stereotypes, "disgusting" and "dirty", which further reinforce their masculine ego; "changing diapers is a woman's job, not a man's." Young children hearing this when their sibling is being changed are forming preconceived notions about what women are supposed to do and what a man's role is in the home. Remember, children are highly impressionable. If you were a young boy and you heard that changing diapers was disgusting, dirty, and a woman's job, would you want to do change diapers when you were married with your own children? Probably not!

Children are taught that certain duties, roles, and tasks are designated to certain genders. Cooking, cleaning, laundry, dishwashing, and sewing are female activities. Cutting the lawn, shoveling the snow, and fixing things are male activities. Perhaps the way most men view task differences is productivity. Since men tend to be more task-oriented, they are more likely to perceive chores in ways which produce results. They are more likely to view cutting the lawn as qualifying the appearance of their home, whereas washing dishes or sewing does not produce the same tangible result which they could rate as a "job well done." Completion of a task and success are what matters most to men, rather than merely performing mundane repetitive tasks. Sons take close notice of their father's attitudes.

Through family socialization, some boys do not want to be like women because of what women are forced to endure: domination, abuse or neglect. Incidences of battered woman syndrome are being reported more today than ever before. Most of these women who are being abused by men have children and the children are witnessing the abuse. What happens to a boy who constantly watches his father abuse or neglect his mother? A boy might grow up fearing or resenting their father. If this is the case, then they are likely to lose respect for their father and identify more with their mother. A second, more probable, occurrence would be boys watching their abusive fathers, identifying their fathers as role models, and disrespecting their mothers the same way their fathers have. They perceive their mothers as weak and helpless, and fathers as strong and powerful. Boys want to be strong and powerful because this is what they are socialized into thinking they should be. Later in life, they are more likely to take what they learned from the way their father treated their mother and apply it to their own relationships. If their father treated their mother poorly, then they are more likely to treat their own wives poorly. If their father treated their mother with respect and had a good, loving relationship with them, then they are likely to form their own healthy, loving relationships. Unfortunately, more of the former seems to be occurring since divorce rates and incidences of domestic abuse are so high. In some families, fathers work six or seven days a week and when they are home, they spend very little quality time with their wives or their children. Even though these fathers are not abusive, they may emotionally neglect the family, and their sons both consciously and unconsciously observe this. When they are old enough to start their own family, many believe that to be a good husband and father means to work as many hours as you can and be the breadwinner. Since the parents never split up or divorced, everything must be "okay" with things the way they were. The sons then carry this attitude into their own marriages.

OWN PERSONAL EXPERIENCES

Some men do not want to be like women as a result of their own personal experiences with wives or girlfriends. If you have had a terrible or horrific relationship with someone, you are not likely to soon forget it. Sane minds would assert the next person you would want to get involved with is not someone like the last. If you don't want to find someone like the one before, you sure as heck don't want to be like that person.

Many divorced men claim their ex-wives were pains in the rear, always nagging them about something. The "something" they were nagging about was usually change. They wanted their husbands to change something in their life, either something annoying that they were already doing, or something desirable that they weren't doing. Usually, men don't change. They are the way they are and are content being that way. Their mothers love them for who they are so their wives should accept and love them all the same.

Most men will say their wives' nagging only made things worse. "The more she nagged, the more I purposely would fight her," he would say. The nagging is perceived as a challenge by men. The more women try to change a man, the more he defies her. As the power struggle continues, he is more likely to recall or be reminded of the negative stereotypes assigned to women who always nag and complain. This further fuels the fire when he tosses sarcastic insults regarding "nagging" in her face.

When all is said and done, he feels he has won even at the loss of a relationship. His competitive nature prevents him from dwelling on the failed relationship. Instead, he focuses on his apparent victory; "she didn't break me." Sometimes losing a wife or girlfriend is perceived as much better than losing one's pride. If he feels he has won, then he also believes she has lost. If she loses the battle, then she is second best. Most men do not want to be second best!

Men do not want to be like women because they push, prod, dig, and nag. They find this very irritating and repulsing. Some would rather lose their relationship than lose the battle of pride. Since men want to win, they can never picture themselves being more like women.

CASE STUDY

Ten year old Mike was asked by his teacher to write a story about what he wanted to be when he grew up. He wrote a story about how he wanted to get married, have a family, and stay at home to raise his kids just like the way his mother raised his sister and him. His teacher was so impressed with his paper that she gave him a gold star. Very proud of his accomplishment, he brought the paper home and showed his mother, who read it and gave him a big hug and kiss to show how proud she was of his perfect paper. His father, who looked at the paper, smiled at his son because he had received a gold star. His wife then made him read it. As he read it, the smile on his face slowly became a frown. He sat there for a moment and stared at the paper before crumpling it into a ball and tossing it into the garbage. Mike stared at him in disbelief as tears welled up in his eyes. "Why did you do that dad? I got perfect on it!" he asked. His father replied, "the only thing you will get perfect on in life is acting like a man and doing what real men do!"

• What parents say to their children is taken to heart. Children believe what their parents tell them. What you tell your children can have a profound bearing on the rest of their lives!

CHAPTER EIGHT

MEN WANT WHAT THEY ALREADY HAD BUT ONLY AFTER THEY'VE LOST IT!

And in the end the love you take is equal to the love you make.

The Beatles, The last lyric of their last song

Many men want what they already had, but only after they've lost it! Men wonder why their wives eventually leave, while believing that pleading and begging all the time was "all right". Why do men want what they already have after they've lost it? Why not appreciate what they have when they have it?

Men are highly visual creatures, whereas women are highly social and verbal beings. Remember in the last chapter, you learned that sons learn from their fathers by observing them. When they are young, boys learn to pay attention to what they see rather than what they hear. Do you have a son? Have you ever seen him watch his favorite baseball star? Notice how he mimics the athlete's batting stance, quirks, and mannerisms. This comes through observation and repetition. Most boys need to see rather than hear to learn.

Visual learning becomes stronger in adolescence for males. Young men begin to pay more attention to how women are dressed. They notice post-pubescent changes in young women. They could be friends with a female their entire life but begin to treat them differently when they notice breasts and curves on a once skinny girl. Girls tend to treat male friends the same way throughout life. It doesn't matter whether it's pre-puberty or post-puberty, girls were attracted to personality and it is the personality they are always drawn to. Boys, on the other hand, can be friends with a girl who has a great personality but when a beautifully developed girl walks into the room, one's personality takes a back seat to appearance.

Have you ever wondered why most men hate romantic love stories? Have you ever noticed how men prefer action movies with large amounts of blood, gore, and violence? Some of this has to do with the cowboy syndrome I discussed earlier. However, most of it has to do with men's preference for visual stimulation. Love stories have a lot of dialogue and intense, intimate moments. Women can relate because for most, this is their true shining quality, the ability to communicate. Remember, men are not the effective communicators women are. Men rely more on sight. They are drawn to fast paced movies with action and intense scenes because it captures their attention. Intimate dialogue does not capture their attention the same way.

Who do you think is more likely to enjoy fresh, juicy gossip: men or women? If you answered women then you are probably right, most of the time. Professional women colleagues of mine have quipped many times they would rather work with a room full of men than women. They often times say women are much crueler than men in what they say. They can be your friend one moment, but stab you in the back the next! On the other hand, a guy can say something cruel or harsh to another guy and he will just shrug it off and say, "whatever." If it does escalate into a fight, they can be beating each other one moment then buying each other drinks the next. Women are more likely to maintain a running feud over what has been said. Why?

Women are verbal creatures who look for connotative meanings with what has been said. Men take things at face value and do not dig down for deep, intended meanings as most women do. Men rely more heavily on what they see. They are the ones who need to see to believe. Most women need to hear to believe. When men don't talk to their wives, women hear what husbands are telling them by their silence: "I can't communicate with you" or "I won't communicate with you."

It is their visual world which often times gets men into trouble. Men are always comparing what they have with what they don't have. Their best friend Bob gets a new car. They compare their old car to Bob's new car. They like Bob's car better so they buy a new car. Their neighbor gets an in- ground swimming pool. They were going to get an above ground pool, but changed their minds because they want the in-ground pool since it "looks better." Men get into most of their relationship troubles for the same reason: vision! They like to look at women.

What do you think is one of the largest entertainment businesses around? Movies? Theater? Sports? Try the pornography industry! This industry has grown to tremendous heights with the introduction of new Internet venues. Who are the largest consumers of pornography? Men. Which men use pornography the most? Married men with families.

The pornography and adult entertainment industry is geared toward men for one main reason: vision. Men become aroused by what they see. Some individuals might assert the reason men get hooked on pornography is because of their sex drives caused by the hormone testosterone. I disagree with this because women do not have the high levels of testosterone produced in their bodies and they still like to have sex. In fact, some women like sex just as much, if not more, than men! The testosterone theory doesn't cut it!

Another example to prove my "vision" explanation is the use of beer commercials. When are they most likely aired? During sporting events. Who is most likely to be watching sporting events and drinking beer? Men. How often have you seen scantily dressed women wearing nothing more than bikinis in these beer commercials? What do bikinis have to do with sports and beer? Absolutely nothing! The only commonality is that men are interested in all three. What do sports and bikini clad women have in common? Men use their eyes to view and become stimulated by what they see.

Most men like the notion of being married. They like the comfort and security of having a wife. After a while, some men need to stimulate their visual senses and look somewhere else. Their wives are like television re-runs: same story, same nagging, different time, same place.

How do men alleviate their visual boredom? They look somewhere else for something to spice up their life. Perhaps they rent a pornographic movie. Perhaps they begin frequenting strip clubs. Maybe they try the services of a prostitute or visit an erotic massage parlor.

As soon as men begin reaching out for new venues, they consciously and subconsciously over-step a boundary and literally open Pandora's box. Like alcohol, drugs, and gambling, sex is also addictive. Some men who get a taste of the adult entertainment world never get satisfied and always need more. When the urge goes on long enough, it eventually becomes an addiction. When the urge to see something sexual or do something sexual becomes an unstoppable addiction, it is definitely going to destroy a marriage.

I am sure most men have been to a strip club or watched a pornographic movie at least once in their lives. I am sure most women have also experienced both as well. It is how the viewer watches sexual acts, which determines how it will affect their lives.

Some people are able to watch sexually provocative mediums and see them as nothing more than entertaining. Others, on the other hand, watch them to fill "something" which they believe is missing in their lives. As a psychology professor, I often times teach courses in criminal psychology. In the criminal psychology courses, I often times cover areas which include the adult entertainment industry. I bring in friends who are police officers to be guest speakers. These police officers often times bring in exotic dancers and former prostitutes to provide profiles of who their typical clients usually are. Their typical clients are married men who are lonely. They claim their wives either don't like to have sex anymore or they "don't understand them." These men in turn look outside of their marriage for fulfillment for what they believe they need.

What is it that men really need? Is it sex? Is it another woman to tell them how great they are? Men need their egos groomed. Some men need to know if they "still got it."

There are perhaps a host of factors which, when paired with temptation, lead men astray. First, let's examine an example of a relationship. A husband's wife is always on his back about something. No matter what he does, she is constantly nagging him to change. Second, he frequently visits a strip club. He has a few drinks and has fun with the women to escape his everyday concerns. When he leaves the bar, he returns to a situation which he perceives as negative and is forever trying to ignore. Then what? Perhaps he begins to make conscious comparisons in his mind about life at home and life at the strip club. The women there don't get on his case. They are always a lot of fun. They make him feel good about himself. He feels like a real man. And the girls are damn attractive! On the other hand, his wife is a nag, which is making her company less attractive and he no longer perceives her as attractive as the "other" women. I used the example of women at the strip club but perhaps it is women he works with, passes in a store, etc.

The key point is that he is noticing other women. Perhaps in the beginning, he would look at them and say to himself, "she's hot." Now he's looking at them and saying , "she's hot and I want her." These "she's" represent the women in the beer commercials who are always getting along and being nice with their men. These "she's" are like the women in the strip clubs who are always a lot of fun. And these "she's" are not mundane, redundant "naggers" his wife represents. At some point, his eyes will wander once too often and he may cross the line of infidelity.

Men are visual creatures, not the communicative creatures women are. When there is a problem in the relationship, women want to discuss it. Men, on the other hand, do not want to talk about it. Why? Because they, "don't see any problems." If they can't see it, then it can't possibly be.

What men perceive is a nagging wife who won't leave him alone. She becomes the enemy who threatens his ego. She picks and prods and inadvertently pushes him away. No matter how hard she tries to communicate with him, he fights her. He doesn't see anything wrong with himself, with what he's doing, or with the relationship.

The more he perceives her as a threat, the more he is going to start to look elsewhere for sanctuary and reaffirmation for who he is. Where is he likely to find it? In the bed of another woman!

Perceived neglect, abuse, or jealousy in a relationship often leads individuals into doing bad things. When men feel inadequate, misunderstood, or threatened, they seek solace in an outside relationship (Bryson & Shettel-Neuber, 1978). As I stated earlier, men do not see "the other woman" as a perceived threat to their vulnerability. She represents a fresh experience in life as opposed to his negative wife. Men can go outside of their marriages and have sex with complete strangers and it means nothing. Men are much more likely than women to enjoy sex without any emotional involvement (Quadagno & Sprague, 1991). Men can separate the emotional part of sex from the physical because they operate in the physical, visual world.

Men can actually have sex with another woman besides their wives and not feel guilty about it. When a married man uses the services of a prostitute, he asserts, "it was only sex." There was no love, no emotional intimacy, or connection.

It was just consensual sex! He was fulfilling a physical need and nothing more. He could see and feel this need being met, but he still loves his wife and would "never do anything to purposely hurt her." He really believes this and in his heart he means it.

Women are dumbfounded at how a man can tell his wife he loves her one moment and jump into bed with another woman the next. It is because he perceives the world differently. For most women, sex and love are part and parcel. For many men, sex and love are independent of the other.

The beer commercials and pornographic movies with the sexy women represent sex and freedom from the married world of love. In the world of "love" there are the responsibilities of being a husband, father, caretaker, and emotional communicator. Sometimes these duties are too overwhelming. Sometimes being an emotional communicator is too difficult or even impossible. How does he cope with it? He enters a world he knows best. He goes to a place which is superficial and simple. What you see is what you get. He chooses to participate in the visual world and let the chips fall where they may. Unfortunately, often times things get out of control and his world of love disintegrates.

CASE STUDY

Cindy works in the adult entertainment industry as an exotic dancer. She has been doing so ever since she was 21 to pay off her university loans. When she first got into the business she swore she would only do it for the money and quit once all of her debts were paid off. She also swore up and down she would never have sex for money with any of the patrons. Funny how things never work out the way you plan them. Cindy is now 30 and still taking her clothes off for money. On several occasions, Cindy has even crossed the line of carnal knowledge with her customers. She is not proud of it, but she says it's a living and it pays the bills. She says she also needs the money to pay off her drinking tabs. When Cindy is asked who her typical clients are that come to watch her dance, she claims they are mostly married man. She further adds they are "lonely" and "unhappy" married men. Are they not having sex with their wives? Many claim it is boring or not the same anymore as it was when they first met. She asks them if they think it is right that they are in a strip joint when their wives and kids are at home. Most respond by saying sure, there is no harm in having a little fun. Furthermore, some who lower the bar and have extra-marital sex claim they are not purposely trying to hurt their wives, rather they are just having "sex." To them, sex is not the same as love because it is just the act of "getting off". What their wives don't know won't hurt them! Cindy ponders their ideas about sex and asks them if they really believe they are doing nothing wrong. She says some think for a moment but overall, sex is just sex and they love their wives and will stay married!

• Can a man or woman have sex outside of their marriage and it mean absolutely nothing? If their spouse or family never finds out, does it hurt the marriage?

CHAPTER NINE

MEN WANT WHAT THEY ALREADY HAD BUT ONLY AFTER THEY'VE LOST IT BECAUSE THEY DON'T LIKE CHANGE

Men always want to be a woman's first love - women like to be a man's last romance.

Oscar Wilde

Men want what they already had, but only after they have lost it! This is because many of them don't like change. In the last chapter, I discussed how a man's wandering eyes, his miscommunication, and misperception can cause his relationship to falter or even dissolve. What happens when his wife leaves him? He wants her back. Sometimes at any cost!

Wives learn, often through repeated trials, that their husbands are not going to change. Men are the way they are and so be it. Interestingly, these "unchangeable" ways prove to be a double-edged sword for some men.

During a relationship or marriage, a man chooses not to change or he simply cannot change no matter how many times his mate encourages him too. He may attempt to change, or just change for the sake of appeasing her, but reverts back to his old ways not too soon after. Just as many men can't change for their mate, they can't change for themselves either.

Some may have an extra-marital affair or weekend romances and fool themselves into believing they have found the woman of their dreams. They see their mistress once or twice a week for some good, down-right, nasty sex. The sex is great and they wish their fun experiences with their mistress could be characteristic of their marriage. It's not. Their mistress represents both an escape from their mundane marriages as well as a sexual rebellion against their wife. "How dare she tell me to change or else she's going to leave...I'll show her!"

When he feels he cannot tolerate his wife's unrealistic expectations for change, he might behave in any of the following ways. If he does have a mistress, he may choose to tell his wife about her and leave. A second thing he might do if he has a mistress is behave in such awful ways as to make his wife leave him so he can then go to his mistress. If he doesn't have a mistress and thinks he could do much better if his wife would leave, he might provoke a situation where she does leave him. Finally, if he doesn't have a mistress, doesn't want to be married anymore, and wants to be alone, then he might continue on as he has done until she tires of him and leaves him. In all of these situations, he consciously pushes the right buttons to set himself free from his marriage.

In the situations where there is a mistress, leaving his wife may prove highly detrimental. Keep in mind that most extramarital affairs are purely physical. They are novel, exciting, and sexual. Once the novelty wears off, as it does in any relationship, the couple evolves toward emotional intimacy. It is at this point that both partners must begin communicating with each other. There are three major problems men encounter:

I

The reason he left his wife in the first place was because she wanted him to change and grow effective communication. His relationship with his mistress is not what it once was. It has become a regular relationship. In essence, he left a loving wife in a proven relationship for the unknown. He is now facing similar expectations he had in his marriage with a woman he hardly knows. The pressures he feels in this new relationship are worse than his marriage. Men like to "win", therefore he has the added pressure of making this relationship work to justify his choice for leaving his wife. He might actually have to take an introspection of himself, which he avoided like skunk spray while married. If he does, he might realize something within himself is broken and needs fixing. In all probability, his ego defense mechanisms will kick in and he will behave as he did with his wife.

II

Since the relationship with his mistress was purely of a sexual nature in the beginning, he has probably mistaken lust for love. Most relationships which start out as purely sexual are often times misinterpreted or manufactured into something they are incapable of ever becoming: love. Women are often times accused of being too fantastical in their perceptions of love and romance. They are sometimes portrayed as getting caught up in the wanderlust of daytime soaps and fairy tales.

Women are more likely to be led with their hearts and then rationalize with their minds about love and romance. Men, on the other hand, are more likely to be led with their hormones and fall in head first before they get a chance to rationalize what has taken place. For this reason, men are more likely to mistake lust for love.

III

If his mistress does engage in a long-term romantic relationship with him after he leaves his wife, will she ever be capable of trusting him? What thoughts would run through your mind if you started a relationship with a man who already had a wife or girlfriend and they left them to be with you? Would you not wonder if and when he might do the very same thing to you? How would you respond? If anything, he is more likely to find his mistress questioning his behaviors more than his wife was because she unconsciously has learned not to trust him. Remember, most women are able to think with their heads and their hearts. The last thing they want is another broken heart so they are going to be on guard.

All three of these problems need consideration. In the first scenario, it will eventually strike him like a cold slap in the face. "What have I done? I left the comforts of a secure relationship, which at times was boring, for an insecure relationship, which is becoming the same way." When both parties are forced to communicate, they will probably realize they have less in common than they ever thought. Sure the sex was great, but it is not enough to sustain a relationship. He may decide to leave his mistress when she begins to nag him or she might beat him to the punch when she sees how predictable and boring he is. Where does this leave him? Probably alone and heartbroken.

In the second scenario, relationships based purely on sex and physical chemistry often times never measure up in the communicative department. Sure, women want great sex, but they also want a man they can communicate with. If he was not able to achieve emotional intimacy with his wife, he is less likely to achieve it with his mistress. If she is seeking a romantic relationship, he had better produce that both in the bedroom and emotionally. If he doesn't, she will also question his manhood.

What if she doesn't want any sort of relationship with him after he has left his wife? Then he really is out of luck! He left his wife for another woman and the other woman sure as guns better take him! He needs to prove to himself that leaving his wife was the right choice. In order to prove this, he needs to establish a relationship with the other woman. If she won't take him then this will be a crushing blow to his ego. He does not want to crawl back to his wife with his tail between his legs.

Lust does not equal love! Those who subscribe to the type of love known as Eros, which sociologist John Lee describes as one based on strong physical attraction, physical perfection, and chemistry, are sure to be disappointed. Lee says, once you get past the sex and start looking for short-comings and imperfections in the other person, you fall out of love. Ironically, you were never "in love" in the first place, rather it was pure lust. Lust does not last because it is not steady and stable. I am guessing many marriages based on erotic love are the first to end in divorce.

The third problem asserts that a mistress who engages in a long-term relationship with a married man is less likely to trust him. If she ever does develop true loving feelings for him, she is likely to keep her guard up. Many times when a married man initiates a long-term relationship with a mistress while he is married or after he has left his wife, he makes a lot of promises. Most men want to have their cake and eat it, too. He doesn't want to lose his wife nor does he want to lose the great sex he is having with his mistress. He begins to give her trinkets, gifts, and personal promises. If she is foolish enough, she accepts his tokens and buys into his promises.

When he eventually does leave his wife, he is probably confident he has some degree of "ownership" over his mistress by what he has given to her. At this point, she probably expects a whole lot more emotionally. He will likely continue to make promises until he knows he has truly won her over. At this point, he will probably revert back to the behaviors he employed in his marriage. If she is perceptive enough, she will see through his ploys and question his actions. Why should she trust him? Would you?

When a man realizes what he has gotten himself into, he is probably going to question himself. Did I make the right choice in leaving my wife to be with my mistress? If his mistress wants nothing to do with him, he is sure to ask himself, "what the heck have I done?"

Where does he go from here? Well, for starters, he is going to wage a mental war with himself. He will repeatedly try to justify his choice as being "right" and may get some satisfaction in believing he won. This satisfaction is sure to dissipate quickly when he realizes he has won nothing more than loneliness.

Have you ever heard the proverbial saying, "absence makes the heart grow fonder"? In his case, absence is going to make him want to kick himself in the backside for being so stupid because he has never felt so miserable.

When a man leaves his wife for another woman, he is incapable of severing all ties to his wife. When the relationship with his mistress does not work out, the first person he usually runs to is his wife. Why on earth would he run back to his wife after treating her the way he did? Does he not have any shame or dignity? Sure, he has both shame and dignity, but what he doesn't have is his wife, his primary caregiver.

Even though his extra-marital affair was exciting and invigorating, it lacked something; real love. His wife was his security blanket, the person he could always depend on. Even though she seemed annoying at times, she was his wife.

What does "wife" mean to most men? Perhaps a pillar of dependability and stability. When he left her for another woman, he lost that. Even if he didn't leave her for another woman, but merely pushed her away because he wanted to be single, he was bound to miss the dependable attributes she offered him.

When men leave their wives, they do so without weighing heavily all of the pros and cons. Most only "see" things at the surface level where momentary gratification is provided. Men don't like change and when they realize their worlds are changing, they need someone who can bring a homeostasis back to their lives. They need someone who represents the way things once were. They need their wives.

As I asserted, most men are lead by what they see rather than what they are truly emoting. Some women claim men think with what is below their waist rather than what is between their two ears! In some situations they make pretty telling cases.

Men want something new but they just don't know what it is! They think whatever it is, it must come from outside. If it is not toys, then perhaps it is another woman. If it is not another woman, then maybe it's solitude. Often times, whatever they choose, it's not what they really wanted. What most men need is to get in touch with their inner beings. They need to know who they are. And to learn who you are, you need to express yourself to someone who will listen. Wives will listen, and want to listen, but men just do not know how to begin. Some may try, but many take the alternate route by running away both physically and psychologically.

When a man tires of running and becomes lonely, he realizes his wife and marriage were most important to him all along. His wife wanted him to change but he didn't want to change. Rather than work with her he worked against her. Even though he left her, he still did not change. It is for this very reason he wants her back. He wants things the way they were!

Most women are capable of change. And because most are, when he tries to win her back she says it is too late. He tries everything to get her back, but she wants nothing to do with him. He says he has learned his lesson and has truly changed. I believe most women have heard this script once too often. They know he hasn't changed. In fact, some women find his desperate attempts at reconciliation silly and pitiful and are even more turned off by the man they were once in love with. There are some wives who can forgive a man who has cheated on them or who has decided he wants to be alone. After long painful hours of soul searching, these women are able to take their husbands back on conditional terms. Most times, however, things go back to the way they once were and wives find it even easier to bring closure to the relationship when he reverts back to his old ways.

Many men who want their wives back really do love them! However, many also want their wives back out of habit and for security. Men who promise to change if their spouses take them back are really fooling no one but themselves. If a man is going to change, it is going to have to occur without his wife pushing or prodding him and watching over him. Someone can only change themselves for themselves. There are men who beg their wives for one more chance and say they want to go for marital counseling, but why? Wives don't need the counseling in situations where he has cheated or run out on her. He needs the therapy! Some men will use the "therapy plan" as a bargaining ploy. Don't buy into it. If he really wants to change, then encourage him to change for himself and wish him well. Those who really are authentic about changing will do so for themselves and give their wives no more grief or heartache.

Men want what they already had only after they lost it because they appreciate it that much more. Sometimes, the best lessons in life are those hardest learned. Men don't like change! Even though things may appear great, novelty has a way of wearing off. When something we cherished is gone, we want it back much more than when we are faced with adversity. Marriage is no different.

CASE STUDY

Sheila discusses how she gave her husband repeated chances to change only to be disappointed:

"We were married quite young. I was 20 and he was 24. We met at a college dance. He really was not my type but he convinced me to go out with him with his persistence, which I found both flattering and kind of cute. After I had my daughter when I was 23, I found out that he had been cheating on me for a couple of years. The scary part was that it was not just with one woman, but many. One of those women was my best friend, who came clean. Eventually, I was able to forgive her. What was really amazing was the fact that I forgave him first! Now that I am 32, I can take no more. We have had one more daughter since then, and he has also had many more lovers.. I am tired of all the deceit and promises to change and to get help. We went to see a marriage counselor a few months ago and it was there that I had the courage to call it quits and finally leave him. He was quite surprised and thought for sure I would cave in and give him yet 'another chance. No dice this time around. I don't know if and when I will ever be able to trust another man again. For now, I am just working on regaining my self-esteem and dignity!"

• Too many individuals know what this type of hurt is like. How many "chances" does it take before you have had enough?

CHAPTER TEN

MEN WANT WHAT THEY ALREADY HAD BECAUSE THEY ARE JUST APPLYING THE RULES OF THEIR PRIOR RELATIONSHIP TO THEIR PRESENT RELATIONSHIP

Love does not consist in gazing at each other, but in looking outward together in the same direction.

Antoine de Saint-Exupéry

Many men want what they already had but only after they have lost it because they are just applying the rules of their prior relationship to their present relationship! Since men don't like change, they don't change their perceptions of their relationships. Many men choose to live in the past because it represents "social comfort".. Men want things the way they once were.

When a wife or girlfriend leaves her mate, he is likely to try and get her back. He tries everything but if she believes he hasn't changed and, in the process, fallen out of love with him, then it's game over!

While I was completing my doctorate years ago, I recall an interesting assertion regarding relationships. Someone once said, "when a woman and man meet and start a relationship, the woman is more likely to fall in love first and it takes the man a while to catch up to her level, sometimes never, or when she decides to leave him." Perhaps this is why many men have a hard time moving on after their relationship with their spouse ends. They don't realize how much they love their wives until they are gone.

Have you ever dated a man who constantly talks about his past relationships? He discusses his ex-mates as if he is obsessed with them. Well, maybe he is obsessed. What he is obsessing about is probably likely to differ. Some men fall in love after the break up and they really are obsessed with getting their ex-wives back. On the other hand, some men are not obsessed with their ex-wives, rather more obsessed by the fact they were dumped. Being dumped means they didn't "win" and they need to go over the game film and figure out why they lost! Both of these situations represent change and both violate the rules many men have about relationships.

When a woman rejects a man, he feels forced into uncharted territory. Often times he has to take a long, hard look at himself, which is not what he wants.

Therefore, he affixes the blame for the relationship failing onto this ex-wife. Earlier I mentioned how men are highly competitive: they need to win! Many look at the finality of a relationship the same way. Even though they sabotaged the relationship, men will try to recover it for the sake of trying. Even if she doesn't take him back, he can tell himself he tried to make things work and she is the one to blame for bailing out.

When I asked you if you have ever met a man who dwells on his past relationships, did he also tell you how much he tried to make things work in his last relationship but his mate still ran out? Did he discuss other relationships that ended the same way? If so, then you begin to notice a pattern. Were all the women he was involved with quitters or is he unchangeable?

Throughout this book I have discussed how most men are set in their ways and do not want to change. They apply these same sets of "unchangeable" rules to each relationship they embark in. They were taught what their fathers were taught and so on. Many generations have created what most men are today: unchangeable!

When a man begins a new relationship fresh out of a failed relationship, he has not had time to heal and resolve his issues. Most times, he uses the new relationship to fill the void of the last relationship. He starts a relationship because he needs to be with someone. The relationship will start out like the last one, full of interest and energy. After a while, he will slip into his complacent, comfort zone when he knows he has her genuine interest. If the pattern holds true to form, he will consciously or unconsciously manufacture a way to chase his new beloved away. He is back to square one. His relationships are very similar to those women who have battered women's syndrome. These women have dependent personalities and need to be in a relationship to get their identity from their mate. Being with a man gives them a sense of self-esteem. Dependent men choose a relationship for much the same reason. The only difference is that men tend to be physical caregivers whereas women are emotional caregivers. Battered women most times seek out men to physically support them. Men from repeated failed relationships seek women for emotional support or, as I asserted earlier, primary caregivers.

Battered women, who often times are co-dependent, have lives that are cyclical. They are alone, find someone who they fall "in love with", and then he beats her and she is alone once again. She looks for another man to take the place of the last one. The cycle repeats itself. Needy men are very similar. They are alone, meet someone who falls in love with them, they push her away, and once again he is alone. Because women readily accept change more so than men, at some point the battered woman is likely to seek professional help and work on her own self-esteem. Men, on the other hand, resist change and perceive the world externally. Rather than admit their personalities and behaviors are the cause of their failed relations, they are more likely to blame their ex-mates. By holding this perception, they are less likely to seek professional help to correct their own self-esteem deficiencies. Instead, they are likely to proceed into another dysfunctional relationship perpetuated by themselves.

Since men are not willing to change, they will continue to apply the gender rules learned early in life with their future mates. There is the adage, "misery loves company." Many men apply this saying to the perceptions they hold about relationships. Anger, which becomes hardened with time because of intense bitterness an individual experiences, is likely to wreck a person's life. Some men are not able to get over a failed relationship and they place irrational blame on their partner. Unfortunately, they carry this blame and anger with them into their next relationship because they have never resolved their embittered feelings. When they carry this anger into their next relationship, they are more likely to unconsciously transfer it onto their partner. By transferring his anger, he becomes more closed-minded, more confrontational, and even more resistant to change. Some men use their aggressive, competitive nature to try and manipulate their partner in their new relationship. When they believe things are out of control, they are likely to feel vulnerable and perhaps afraid. When they begin to feel this way, their defenses kick in and they view the relationship as a challenge.

His mate represents the other women who he believes have hurt him in the past. He plays to win! How does he do this? The same way he did in the past. He resigns from her or pushes her away, or he seeks out a mistress to try to gain some sense of control over the relationship. In fact, the only thing lacking in control is himself and his irrational perception for dealing with the relationship causes it to spiral downward.

Where does this leave his significant other? She may question her own self-esteem and competence as a woman since she can't understand why their relationship does not grow. Also, she might decide she has had enough and leaves him. He is back to square one!

Men want what they already had only after they have lost it because they need a sense of control. Control means stability, and they seek out women who they think will follow their relationship "rules". Men lack communicative skills women possess and they wind up experiencing very tough, painful lessons. Unfortunately, many men do not learn from their lessons. All relationships have implied rules. Like anything in life which has rules, the rules must be applicable and acceptable by all parties involved. Men who repeatedly fail in relationships have their own set of rules and women are expected to cooperate. When they don't cooperate and deviate from what is expected of them, women are then perceived as "bitches."

CASE STUDY

Tony has what is called independent personality disorder. It is more common in males. Tony is an individual who always exaggerates his sense of sureness and personal power. Whenever he is in a relationship, he emphasizes his lack of need for others. He constantly tells his girlfriends he is able to live without others forever. Well, this happens while his mate is still in his life.

Whenever Tony feels his relationship slipping away, he becomes obsessed with the need to control the object of his jealousy; his mate. He is constantly driven by his anger, which is caused by an irrational fear of being abandoned. Tony has very distorted thoughts about what love is. He has always been a "pusher-puller" in all his relationships ever since he can remember. The closer someone gets to Tony, the more he withdraws from them and pushes them away. When they finally start to take his cue and leave him, he begs them to come back to him and give him another chance. This method of operating in his relationships has plagued Tony for nearly 20 years now. At 36 years of age, he is finally seeking professional counseling to try and change his approach to relationships.

• The way we treat others in relationships is usually a great reflection of the relationship we had with our parents growing up. In Tony's childhood, his father always worked while his mother stayed at home. He rarely witnessed public displays of affection between his parents and his father always taught him that being a breadwinner is the most important thing in life. Tony never had a very close relationship with his mother. In fact, as a child he sometimes used to believe she was a "distraction" to his father.

CHAPTER ELEVEN
MEN ARE THE WAY THEY ARE: A RECAP

Bachelors know more about women than married men; if they didn't, they'd be married too.

H. L. Mencken

Men are the way they are because they are products of societal stereotypes. Furthermore, they are products of these societal stereotypes because their fathers were, their grandfathers were, and so on. It's been going on for generations and it is not likely to change in the very near future.

Men are very different from women for a number of reasons:

1) MEN DON'T LIKE CHANGE

Men are quite content being the way they are. They have been this way their entire lives. Why change? What does it mean when a man has to change for a woman? His psychological parent, passed down from his father, tells him he is not a man if he allows his wife to push him around. She is not trying to push him around, she is only trying to do what she is good at: communicate her true feelings and concerns about the relationship. He interprets change as being bad and himself as being bad. Eric Byrne discussed roles people play in their lives at different times: the parent, the child and the balanced adult. In the parent role, you behave as your parents did and act in ways accordingly. You tend to use words like "should" and "must" in your dialogue. These words imply power over another. In the child role, you behave irresponsibly like a child. There are times when you play the child role in acceptable situations like fun and games, but often times you behave immaturely when you should be more responsible. The balanced role is where you are in your current state of mind and you behave as the situation dictates. When women assert that their men change, they are perceived by men as being in the parent role. When a woman "shoulds" them, they feel as if she is wielding power over him. If she is in the parent role then he perceives himself being in the child role, being spoken down to. When this occurs, he behaves like a child, possibly throwing a tantrum and fights her. Men do not like change!

2) MEN DON'T LIKE TO FEEL VULNERABLE

The answer to the question: what does it mean when a man has to change for a woman? Vulnerability! In being told he has to change or needs to grow, he perceives his partner as labeling his short-comings. Most people do not like correction or accept criticisms readily. When criticisms come from someone we love, it is even more difficult. The parent-child roles play heavily in the perception of the relationship. If there has been any unresolved shame from his childhood or young adult life, when you ask him to change you are opening up his can of shame. Even though he is older and wiser today, the feelings harboring deep down are adamant and he feels today as he did then. You can try to bring to his attention what you perceive as being wrong, but when he perceives you as a threat, his rage will come to the surface to guard against any shame. Remember, men are taught at an early age what pride is and what it feels like. For many, it is more important to have their pride left intact than to be with their significant other.

3) MEN ARE HIGHLY COMPETITIVE

Men are taught at a young age that "winning is everything." Unfortunately, many take this mentality and apply it to their relationships. Is it better to give in to your partner's wishes and still have a partner, or is it better to risk losing your relationship to prove a point? Some men believe in the former! For some, fighting their mates proves they are not weak nor a loser. There is the adage "it's not whether you win or lose, but rather how you play the game that is important." Remember, men perceive the world in quantifiable terms; end results. Does anyone ever remember the loser in each Superbowl? I have heard questions asked many times by men, who also perceive life the same way. It's not as important how you play the game, as long as you win. Some men will say and do anything to win the heart of a woman. Unfortunately, many only play for the wedding day but forget the marriage part!

4) MEN ARE TASK ORIENTED

Many men perceive themselves and relationships as projects. All projects have a beginning and an end. All projects also have a middle where the quality of work is put in. Men see the quantifiable finished product; themselves or the relationship. They perceive change as measurable. In order to measure change, they recount the time and effort they put into a relationship. When their mate asks them to grow, they count days and weeks rather than the quality of happiness. Sometimes we are so caught up in just living, we neglect to see how it is we are actually living. Relationships are never ending projects requiring work.

5) MEN ARE VISUAL

Media relies heavily on the visual senses of men. Sex sells! Men often times are led with their eyes rather than their hearts. Some are forever comparing what they have; wives or girlfriends to what they see on television, strip clubs, and what other men have. Sometimes they don't keep their eyes in check and they cross the line.

6) MEN ARE PRODUCTS OF THEIR PASTS

Fathers make sons what they are today: men. What are men? Perhaps some women would call them creatures of habit with no hope for ever growing emotionally. Men are socialized into being masculine and non-communicative.

They are taught to keep their emotions in check and play the strong, silent type. Furthermore, men are taught to play the traditional, stereotypical gender roles and personalities; breadwinner, baby-sitter, aggressive, and competitive. Many men never truly find out their true meaning in life. When I refer to meaning I am talking about their own identity. They are taught by fathers, coaches, and teachers how to succeed and be the best they can possibly be. Many are caught up living out scripts created by society. Today, more men are actually crossing gender career barriers and becoming nurses, day care workers, and house fathers. A decade ago this would have been frowned upon and in some societies, it still is to this day.

7) MEN LACK INTIMACY SKILLS

Since men are products of their past, many are never taught how to communicate effectively. Many men confuse sex for affection and emotional intimacy. When a wife complains her marriage is lacking intimacy, men are likely to take her comment as an attack on his own sexuality. Men never really developed their intimacy skills and feel threatened when confronted with them.

8) MEN ARE MORE MASCULINE THAN ANDROGYNOUS

Even though gender roles in society are slowly changing, many men continue to fight the change. Women get an early start on playing the androgynous role because as kids they were allowed to be themselves. Men, on the other hand, were plucked away by their fathers and taught exclusive masculine roles. Many men still confuse androgyny with "femininity", which is usually associated with weakness.

9) MEN DON'T WANT TO BE LIKE WOMEN

Most men do not want to be like women because of the negative connotation "womanhood" holds. For some, being a woman means being weak and second best. For others, being a woman means being a "nag", "busybody" and "ultimate pain in the rear." When asked to play the androgyny role, men say "no way" because in their minds this would make them appear like women.

10) IF IT ISN'T BROKEN, DON'T FIX IT

Men who go through repeated failed relationships are often quick to blame their ex-mates as the primary cause. Most men won't change because they believe there is nothing wrong with them. The only time these men are likely to seek counseling help is to win their wife back or save their marriage. Most men only realize a problem exists after it is too late.

This is a recap of why men differ in their perceptions of relationships. The majority of the time you can bet the reason for failed relationships a man experiences is a result of one of these factors. Keep in mind all relationships require two partners and it is not always the man's fault. Just as both contributed to the relationship progressing, most times both partners also contribute to the failure in a relationship.

The key ingredient in any relationship is communication. Whether you are a man or a woman, if you are not willing to communicate, your relationship will not evolve.

CASE STUDY

Neil and Connie have been married for 4 years. Lately, Connie has reached her boiling point and tells Neil if he doesn't shape up, she is out of here! She claims he is worse than their 2 year old son. Connie is constantly picking up after both of them. Connie works full-time as a legal assistant, while Neil works casually in construction. The two come for counseling and for the first part of the session, Connie has been venting about all of Neil's short-comings, which she perceives as the cause of the breakdown in the marriage. Neil tells the therapist he is the same man today as he was when Connie met him. Connie agrees with Neil but asserts that's the problem! Neil was so much fun, a guy who liked to drink, party, and be merry. In fact, Connie's mother warned her she would have her hands full with him. Connie believed he would "grow up" in the marriage. Furthermore, she believed once they had children he would grow into the father role. It didn't happen as she had planned. At 27 years old, Connie claims Neil is the same guy he was at 21. Neil says one of the biggest problems is that Connie is always ordering him around and telling him what to do. He claims to have developed a deaf ear to her. Also, he asserts the more she nags him, the more he tries to defy her. If she is going to keep comparing him to their 2 year old and if she is going to keep acting like his mother, then he is certain to deny her. Neil says he loves his wife and family, but is tired of being "told" to grow up. Because he is always "being told", he believes the only way he feels remotely like an adult in his own home is to defy her and show her he has a mind of his own!

• Women who believe they can change men are in for bitter disappointment. In fact, anyone who thinks they can change someone or that someone will change for them will be greatly disappointed the majority of the time. The more you try to force someone to change, the less likely they will!

CHAPTER TWELVE
HOW WOMEN CAN DEAL WITH THE FACTS

A man who marries a woman to educate her falls a victim to the same fallacy as the woman who marries a man to reform him.

Elbert Hubbard

Now that you have the facts about men, what can you do with them? Perhaps I should paraphrase this question to ask, "what do you want to do about your own relationship?"

There are four realistic possibilities for women already committed to a relationship. The first possibility is that you have a wonderful relationship with your man and communication is at a premium. You find yourself very much in love with your mate and you love him like a best friend. Communication and intimacy are wonderful. Most importantly, neither of you are afraid of growth or change. In fact, you find your relationship becomes stronger whenever unforeseen forks in the road arise. Together, you work things out and your bond becomes that much stronger!

If it isn't broken then don't fix it! When something is good it's that way because it is good. The relationship is strong because of the internal variables which foster it; you and your mate. You don't need any outside advice or interference tampering with something which is solid. A relationship is not an art project. Aesthetics mean nothing. Love and intimacy count. You've got it, so keep it!

The second possibility is to do what many of you have done probably since meeting your "knight in shining armor"; ignore the problem or hope it will go away. I believe women are better "pretenders" than men. Men call experiences in life as they see them and say it as it is. You pretty much know what you are getting with a man. Women, on the other hand, are pretenders. When women are in precarious relationships with men, many pretend the problem doesn't exist or hope it will go away. They like to think men will one day see the light like a ton of bricks hitting them on the side of the head and change. Women are wishful thinkers who pretend their man has changed for the sake of appearances. Even though they know he hasn't changed, inside they hold on to the torch of hope that he will.

What possibility are women faced with who think this way? Go on and pretend nothing is wrong or believe he is going to change. If everything else is working in the relationship (children, house, car, vacations, career, etc.), why should you care that there is no communication or intimacy? Do you care? If you're reading this book, then I am assuming you care big time! In fact, you are sick of pretending and hoping things will change. Consciously, you've come to the conclusion things will never change and will possibly even get worse. Where does this lead you if you're tired of pretending?

You can leave him and bid him adieu. Tell him you are fed up with his antics and need something new. You've given him enough chances to change and there is no use in flogging a dead horse. You leave! Perhaps you can try the last possibility, which is the most diplomatic but also requires time, effort, and perseverance by both. The possibility I am referring to is a course in communication, marital counseling, or some kind of marital retreat facilitated by a trained professional.

I am sure you have pondered these possibilities over many times. You have probably had family and friends suggest these options as well. They seem so simple yet they work. Nothing else has worked, has it? If you don't have a good relationship then you are probably sick and tired of pretending and hoping for change. Moreover, you might be grasping for straws at this point, even contemplating ending the relationship for good.

There is the old adage, "what do you have to lose?" In a relationship which has deteriorated, you have both everything and nothing to lose. You have invested time, emotion, spirit, finances, and the whole gambit of blood, sweat, and tears.

You have invested everything only to find out there is next to nothing left in the relationship. You can pack it in now or you can go that one last step and seek outside help. At this point you have nothing to lose! If you try and it fails you know you have tried everything humanly possible and you can walk away from the relationship with a conscious piece of mind. All too often, some women punish themselves emotionally for failed relationships which weren't their fault. Keep in mind, however, you are not seeking outside help to give you a piece of mind should things not work out but rather to save a relationship with the person you love. It's important you try to save the relationship for the right reason: having a good relationship. If you take the attitudinal approach and try to save it to come out a martyr, it will eventually fail.

Relationships should be saved for the purpose of having a relationship because you love the other person and want to be with the other person. If you try to save a relationship for the sake of saving it, things will further deteriorate. Do it because you want to and because you don't want to let go of love...at least not just yet!

Admitting there is a problem in a marriage or a relationship is very similar to an alcoholic admitting they have a drinking problem. Admitting the problem often times is the paramount task to the road to recovery. The second part of the formula is just as hard: getting the help and making the changes needed. The alcoholic is one person and they alone admit they have the problem, then seek the help they need. In tumultuous relationships, there are two parties and two egos. Often times, only one admits to or recognizes the problem. Getting both parties on the same page is very difficult. Face it, if you were on the same page in the marriage, things wouldn't have deteriorated to what they are now. There was a down-sided progression in the relationship because you are both at different levels of growth. The one who has grown is not afraid of change. The one who has grown is most likely to recognize the problem and knows change is needed. Convincing the other change is needed is going to be like convincing an alcoholic in denial they have a drinking problem. Remember, men don't like change and are very reluctant to it. The idea of outside help is probably going to strike a blow to the male ego. Keep in mind, it is your relationship, too, and you have the right to make whatever suggestions you deem needed.

How do you approach someone who does not want to change? What can you say to him that will lead him to seek outside help with you? How can you come across as non-threatening, non-patronizing, and non-condescending? Over the years, I have worked with many couples and individuals in counseling. Often times, women in bad relationships come to me even though their mates won't. The question I am asked most of the time is, "how can I get him to come to counseling with me?"

Many of these women are frustrated with their husbands and many are on their last leg in the marriage. If their husbands would only open their ears when their wives were speaking, they wouldn't be coming to me months later begging for ways to get their wife back, who has finally left them for good. The best approaches I can suggest for dealing with your mate are simplistic and very humanistic. They take into account both gender differences and the reluctance to change. Try them because, hey, what do you have to lose?

COMMUNICATIVE TECHNIQUES

1) Be Precise

Many times when men are asked to communicate they misinterpret what is being asked of them. Rather than asking men something general like, "how do you feel?", be more specific; "how do you feel about our marriage?" Rather than tell him first what you think is wrong, put the ball in his court and ask him to tell you what he thinks is wrong with the relationship or if it is okay. Males like to initiate and like to be in control. They feel less threatened if they initiate the problem solving. If you come across as a "know-it-all" and appear to accuse him of being the problem then he will argue, withdraw, or rebel against you. If he is allowed to assert what is won, then go with it. Don't be a pushover, but keep in mind this may be the one and only time you get him to open up and express himself. It may be underhanded, but you are in control by asking questions even though they are non-threatening. Remember Socrates, the famous ancient philosopher? He was viewed as the wisest man of his time. Socrates never gave answers, but rather asked non-threatening questions which sought the truth. This same technique is used by successful lawyers who let witnesses hang themselves by getting caught up in their own answers. I am not suggesting you be Socrates or an attorney and "fry" your mate with your line of questions. I am suggesting a non-threatening, diplomatic approach which allows him to open up in his own way and express himself. People like to talk about themselves and the best way to get them to is to ask pertinent questions.

2) Be Assertive

To be assertive is to get what you want or desire without infringing upon or taking away the rights of another individual. Assertiveness is not the same as aggression. Aggression is walking over another person to get what you want.

Often times, women who behave assertively are referred to as "bitches." So what? Women have come a long way and have the right to speak up and get what they want. Why should there be a double standard? If men can be assertive, and many are aggressive, then why can't a woman be assertive? Too many women fall into the passive behavior types where they never get what they want and have their rights taken away. Too many women play traditional roles in relationships and fall prey to aggressive men who don't care about their needs. To be assertive is to stand up for one's self. To be assertive is to be honest, open, and confident. If you don't like the way your relationship is, you have the right to change it. You have the right to voice your opinion and make your requests. He has the right to ignore you, but you have the right to take whatever action you deem appropriate.

3) Listening Empathetically

To listen empathetically is to listen with an extra ear. Hearing one speak is not the same as listening to them. Empathetic listening is a skill which develops and evolves over time with practice. Women tend to be better empathetic listeners than men. To listen empathetically is to understand what one is feeling. Unfortunately, many men do not communicate their feelings, but rather their thoughts. They stay at a surface level. Women need to listen to the denotative surface message men are telling them. When you ask him how his day was and he responds, "okay", he is telling you it was just okay on the surface. Pay attention to his body language, facial expressions, and non-verbal communication. His "okay" might mean, "I want to talk but I just don't know how." After a while, many of us get caught up in habitual listening where he listens to and responds the same way all the time. If he responds work was "okay" each and every day, you start to turn off the extra ear and miss out on the subtle cues. You don't pay attention to his non-verbal messages and he may think you don't care. When you want to start a meaningful conversation about his day hours later, he feels slighted because he needed to talk when he wanted too, but felt you shrugged him off. Yes, men think and behave this way. Men are not good communicators with their emotions.

They've never been taught to express themselves or use reflective listening skills as women have. Keep in mind, if you live with someone who does not have these skills, you may get caught up in their habits and stop empathizing. Therefore, pay attention to your extra ear and listen for meaning. This gives both, you and him, the chance to create expressive conversations.

4) Seek Clarification

To seek clarification is the next step in asking meaningful questions. We ask questions to learn, rather than to judge or patronize. The best way to seek clarification for something you are unsure of is to repeat to the person what you have just heard. Don't assume anything. Do you know what happens when you assume? Clarification is a major component for being empathetic. It allows you to further understand where someone is coming from without judging them. A great way to clarify is to paraphrase. If someone told us they were upset with us, we might respond by saying something like, "it seems like I must have done something wrong or said something hurtful because you seem agitated." Paraphrasing allows the conversation to free-flow to its desired point.

Many relationships have fallen apart or have become difficult situations because they lacked clarification. You need to make sure you are hearing what it is you thought your mate was saying. Always clarify when you're uncertain and do so diplomatically. Like questioning, clarifying might pose a threat for your mate. Try and sound interested and non-blaming. If your mate feels threatened they will retreat or respond harshly and sarcastically. Clarification shows the other, as well as yourself, that you care.

5) Try To Be Non-Threatening

Often times when men are questioned about something, they take it personally. For example, your husband is a half-hour late for dinner and you are seething mad. He comes in the door and you are ready to explode. The first thing out of your mouth is, "why are you late again?" He interprets your question punitively and condescending. In his mind he is saying, "I've got a mother, who the hell do you think are questioning my lateness?" The storm is brewing and another night is destined to be ruined. When you have a problem with his behavior or something he has said, try to state things from your point of view. Most importantly: own your feelings! When he comes home a half-hour late, state your interpretation of the event to him: "I am really annoyed that you are late again. You could have called to tell me you were going to be late. I feel like my time and effort is not appreciated. I feel you don't care about me anymore!"

If you study this statement closely there is no finger pointing or hidden accusations. You assume ownership for your feelings and don't give him any credit for getting you upset. Also, you don't belittle him and try to get even by treating him like a child. Most men have weaker egos than women when it comes to accusations. Most men perceive their wives like they perceive their mothers; women who love them unconditionally and don't berate them. When you question his lateness you question his integrity and freedom. He feels backed into a corner because he perceives you as parent and himself as child. He is going to come out with blazing guns to defend himself. By asking him in a non-threatening manner, you allow him to explain himself and you are more likely to get a sincere apology from him. Also, you have told him how upset you are and that you feel he doesn't care. This might be the ear opening statement he needs to hear from you to let him think about how important you really are to him.

6) Rome Wasn't Built In A Day

Men were not socialized into becoming what they are overnight. They were trained and through trial, error, and repetition they were made into "masculine" males. And what do you know about masculine males? They are not very good communicators. They are afraid to express themselves because it might show vulnerability and weakness. They are highly competitive beings who don't shy away from confrontation. What can you do?

If you want to work on your relationship you better be ready to be very patient. You are not going to undo things overnight. Some men will be more open to change and growth than others. It's important you don't force the issue and nag them to death. If you do, they will fight you. Try doing and saying little things through the course of a day in an assertive manner. What you want to do is get your spouse to open up to you and communicate. You want him to know you value him and the relationship. People can be re-conditioned. If you want people to behave a certain way, then you treat them the way you want them to be. Simply put: kiss him with kindness. You are hoping for a trickle effect. I have seen this when counseling families where all members chose to come for counseling, except the father. I can't help the father because he is not at the session. Who I can help are those who are there. The best way to counsel a family is to treat them as a unit, a whole made up of the sum of parts. Each personality is a part. If each personality decides to change their behaviors and act differently, the whole begins to change its appearance. If dad chooses not to come to counseling, the rest of the family can still benefit and change. When they start to change and behave differently, it will eventually begin to effect dad both consciously and unconsciously. If he wants to keep up with the rest of the Joneses, he too is going to have to modify his existing behaviors, too. Does it work? Most of the time, yes, since the one person who refuses to be counseled is a minority and will eventually have to conform to the majority norm.

Marriage is the same way. If you behave differently and get rid of the character he has become habituated to, then eventually the stone will make ripples in his water and he will feel the waves. When he feels the wave, he is going to modify himself even though he avoids change like the plague. You can't control or change him, but you can yourself! If he learns you can't be controlled and will no longer be compromised, then he will have to follow suit.

CASE STUDY

Tracy has always been in relationships since she was a young teen. She always felt the need to have a boyfriend. When she was 5, her father left her mother for another woman and since then, her mother has been re-married 4 times. At 29, Tracy finally decided to get married to a man 17 years older than her. She has been married for 3 years now and she just had a child. Since giving birth, Tracy has been suffering from depression. Originally, it was thought to be post-partum depression. Since going to a support group for new mothers, she has learned a lot about herself, her past, and the fact that her depression is caused by feeling trapped in a marriage she doesn't want to be in. Tracy fell in love with the idea of being in love. She believes she got married for all of the wrong reasons. The biggest thing she learned is that she always got into relationships because of loneliness instead of being single for a good reason; finding her identity. She feels absolutely horrible she is not in love with her husband. The fact of the matter is she loves him like a father, the one she never had! For the sake of her child she is not going to bail out of the marriage. She believes this commitment is the one true thing she needs to see through in her life. No matter what is takes, she will learn to love her husband the way he should be loved!

- How many times have women had a child quickly with a man, or rushed into a marriage only to have to grow into the marriage? Many women are still led to believe success in life largely hinges on being married and having children. Men and women both need to wait and take a relationship in stride and eventually marry their partner for all of the right reasons. Too many people feel trapped in a marriage and that is not what marriage was meant to be!

CHAPTER THIRTEEN

UNDERSTANDING MEN AND WOMEN TOGETHER

The course of true love never did run smooth.

William Shakespeare

Women, who are very empathetic and intuitive by nature, are perhaps expecting too much from most men, who possess neither of these characteristics. You'll hear men say things about women in their lives like, "you'd swear she could read my mind" or "to live with her you have to be a mind reader." Men are not too far off the mark with these statements. Women are more in tune with the world around them. Women observe non-verbal communication cues most men miss. They can tell you a great deal about another person they have never formally met, but have merely observed. This is why when they ask you something specific as, "where were you?", you answer them and they say "I don't believe you." They already know you are not being honest with them before you even open your mouth. Body language gives you away.

Remember, they have watched and studied males most of their lives.

Some males have the ability to "read" as well However, most males do not analyze their observations the same way women do. Women tend to be more analytical in their observations and categorize things as to make sense of what is going on around them. Men, on the other hand, are more likely to take things at face value.

Women want what they can't have: a male, who is a reasonable facsimile of their fantasy, i.e., their ideal man. In the absence of their "ideal man", women will accept a man who they believe is workable yet changeable.

Some women choose to play the "sculptor role" and shape a man into what they want him to be, or they take on the "savior role", whereby they try to correct his short-comings or destructive behaviors and make him her "ideal man." Many women throw themselves into these roles, thus selling themselves short. You can either stay single forever or get involved with a male who doesn't meet your criteria and try to help him change, or hope he changes on his own.

Women often believe they can change negative characteristics, or they hope negative ideals will magically disappear with time. Women say "I thought he would outgrow it" or "I thought if he really loved me he would change."

The conscious or unconscious desire to change one's mate is an illusion. No one ever changes for another person. If a person does change, he changes for himself, usually motivated by fear or self-gain. Individuals change because they may gain something or lose something. Therefore, they are motivated to change for themselves in order to achieve a means to an end; themselves.

The last reason men are not willing to change is because they believe they are fine the way they are. After all, he's been this way his whole life and the way he was suits him fine. Furthermore, his wife married him as he was, why should he change now?

Many man have not been able to accept the liberation of women. Notice how the word "change" appears in most situations which involve acceptance and adaptation. What women really want is a man who is willing to keep up with her and who is not threatened by change. She wants a man who will be her intimate growth partner. She doesn't want to be placed on a pedestal or taken for granted.

She wants a male partner who is willing and able to share the power equally. She wants a man who is sure of himself and not afraid to share his dreams, fears, deepest wishes, and vulnerabilities. She wants a male partner who will be her best friend. In essence, she wants someone like her.

Many men want what they have had in the past, or whatever is meaningfully symbolic. Unlike females, men tend to be creatures of habit and are content with what they have. However, men are willing to jeopardize their state of contentment at certain times because they feel what they have is not what it really should be. When he started dating his future wife he couldn't wait to have sex with her. She was everything he wanted. He was courteous, charming, endearing, and a "real gentleman." Now that they have been married for a few years, things have changed. She notices he is no longer the way he was when they were dating or when they first got married. Why? He has become content and believes he has little to do with working on the marriage. She begins to prod him for answers and communication. He perceives it as nagging. She seems like the greatest pain in the ass he has ever known. He starts to compare what he has with what is out there.

What happens when someone better comes along? Is she really that much better than what he already had? Is it worth giving up everything for a roll in the hay? Why another woman?

She symbolizes freedom. A freedom in its truest sense, freedom to make decisions on his own, which he may have perceived as being taken away. This is a kind of freedom to feel the novelty of a different situation and it represents a freedom from commitment and meaningful conversation.

Where does this leave men? Men want what they already had but were too foolish to realize it. He wants a woman who understands him in the way he wants to be understood but when she probes, he runs from her. He runs to another woman who he thinks understands him, often times only to become more confused. When he realizes it is his wife he truly loves and needs and it is she who truly understands him, he returns to her. Most times, however, it is too late and she has moved on. Even though he originally rejected his wife by having the affair, he feels the worst of rejection in the end. Likely, his self-esteem is crushed and he needs to reaffirm himself by engaging in another relationship.

In essence, he believes he must undo being rejected by his wife, his emotional caregiver. He needs to find another emotional caregiver!

For many men, if they would communicate and listen to what their wives were trying to tell them, they would save themselves a lot of grief, hardship, and attorney fees. Most times, the message a man's wife is sending him is that she loves him. Unfortunately, he misinterprets her love and affection as a threat to his freedom.

Many men have misconceptions regarding what intimacy is. Men connote intimacy with physical sex or lust. Many mediums have led men to believe sex and lust are the end-all for the achievement of true intimacy. Men believe this is what intimacy is and once they have "made love" to their wives, they have fulfilled their "intimate obligations."

Men and women view "friendship" differently. When discussing the concept of "friendship" with many males, they will often refer to their male buddies as their "best friend" even though they have a wife. On the other hand, when discussing the same issue with women, many will cite their husbands as their best friend and their girlfriends as best friends as well. Many men view marriage and friendship as two distinct entities. They equate friendship with buddies and marriage with wives.

Many men tend to perceive marriage as a transition from bachelorhood to incarceration because of the new responsibilities and the freedoms they feel they are being forced to abandon. One of the reasons I believe men have difficulty in describing wives as "best friends" is they view the wife and marriage as a threat to their freedom.

Interestingly, it is in the way you look at things which gives things meaning. Men and women look at marriage differently, and that is why gender differences exist even in perceptions of marriage.

CASE STUDY

Jim likes to describe his marriage the following way:

"I have been married for 12 years now. We have two children, both boys; an eight year old and a 6 year old. We have a good marriage. I work 6 days a week at the most while my wife stays at home and cuts hair part-time for a living. I still play hockey with the guys a couple nights a week and still go out drinking on the weekends. I let my wife go out with the girls every couple weeks. She likes to go dancing and chat with the girls. Heck, baby-sitting the boys is not that bad! My best friend Mark comes over and we catch a game on the tube and have a few beers and order a pizza or something. I have never had the need or desire to cheat on my wife. Why? Well, she is the mother of my kids and cheating is wrong to begin with. Even if I could cheat behind her back, I wouldn't be able to hide it. Nah, one woman is enough for me. Besides, who else would want an out-of-shape truck driver like me?"

• How do you feel about a spouse who views a marriage this way? If it works, then should there be any tinkering with it? What happens if Jim's wife wants more in their marriage? Do you think he would be able to adapt to the changes she desires? Keep in mind, every marriage is different and what brings happiness and contentment to one may mean chaos to another. I guess whatever works best works if both are in agreement! It is when one wants more that the proverbial "boat" gets rocked and things change!

CHAPTER FOURTEEN

WHAT TYPE OF LOVER ARE YOU?

Love is patient, love is kind. It does not envy, it does not boast, it is not proud. {5} It is not rude, it is not self-seeking, it is not easily angered, it keeps no record of wrongs. {6} Love does not delight in evil but rejoices with the truth. {7} It always protects, always trusts, always hopes, always perseveres. {8} Love never fails. But where there are prophecies, they will cease; where there are tongues, they will be stilled; where there is knowledge, it will pass away. {9} For we know in part and we prophesy in part, {10} but when perfection comes, the imperfect disappears. {11} When I was a child, I talked like a child, I thought like a child, I reasoned like a child. When I became a man, I put childish ways behind me. {12} Now we see but a poor reflection as in a mirror; then we shall see face to face. Now I know in part; then I shall know fully, even as I am fully known. {13} And now these three remain: faith, hope and love. But the greatest of these is love.

1 Corinthians 13 NIV

What type of individual do you consider yourself to be? Are you satisfied with the type of people you are meeting? Bottom line: Do you really understand yourself?

I often give lectures, seminars, and workshops on body language and personality. Body language comprises the majority of messages and signals we give others. Non-verbal communication tells others so much about you before you even begin to talk. Through body language, you reveal so much about your personality. In fact, you become a magnet to attract men who possess the personality traits which will feed off of yours!

In class, students and I discuss the various types of personalities or behaviors women hold when they approach relationships. In examining various personality tests and aptitude tests, I came up with a list I consider to see very characteristic in women who experience repeated bad relationships. David P. Celani does a tremendous job of explaining why battered women return to abusive men in his book, Illusion of Love. I found that some of the same qualities in abused women are found in those who have repeated bad relationships and they always leave wondering what went wrong.

There are no clear-cut mathematical equations or chemistry formulas for why some women act these ways, but there are many similar behavioral qualities which lay credence to these relationship types. What type are you?

TOMCAT LOVER

Are you the type of woman who likes the prototypical "bad-boy"? Do you find your men too boring and just too practical? Do you like the guy with the tattoos, dressed in leather, with a record of past relationships which reads like something from television's most cheekiest soap opera? Do you like the deep, dark mysterious guy you never see in public in the day, but only roams the dance clubs at night? This is the type of guy your parents warned you about. Furthermore, this is the type of guy you gave your friends grief for getting involved with in the past. What makes you different? Do you really think you can change him and mold him to fit your criteria?

The chances of changing this guy are like the chances of trying to cage a wild lion and teach it to become tame like a domesticated house cat. Sure, in the beginning the chase is fun! You like his rebellious style, his immaturity and carefree attitude lets you escape your real world. He is so much fun and exhilarating, a far cry from the "yawners" you went out with in the past. As the relationship begins to evolve, you are about the only thing which evolves as well.

He is always a few miles behind you and just can't grasp the concept of "responsibility." Eventually, you find yourself longing for more; a real man! The one who is more practical and has his priorities straight.

The question you have to ask yourself is; are you now ready for that type of relationship? Your thinking might have been somewhat clouded when you chose the tomcat, but are you willing to let that go and move on?

Remember, most of us are creatures of habit and fall into repetitious snares. Did you fall into one of those snares and take some of the qualities of the tomcat into your personal life? Choosing another tomcat will only make matters worse. Always remember that tomcats don't change. More importantly, you can't change them!

FLORENCE NIGHTENGALE

Have you always longed to be a martyr? Are you the type who can't say no when you really want to? Are you guilty of taking stray cats and dogs into your home? Are you most likely to bring stray men into your life?

When I refer to stray men here, I am referring to those who have absolutely little or no direction in their lives. They have been under mom's thumb and have migrated from woman to woman in hopes of finding a new surrogate mother. Are you their next surrogate mother?

There is nothing wrong with caring about people. It is wrong, however, to literally take care of a grown man whom you allow to take advantage of you. Women who behave this way are likely to get walked all over and in the end lose both a sense of self as well as materialistic belongings.

I believe women who are attracted to men who require childlike care are those who were taught nurturing roles at an early age. They might have been forced to take care of their younger siblings or a parent with an illness. They have pretty much played this nurturing role throughout their lives. Taking care of someone helps give them a sense of identity as well as meaning in their life. Each stray cat becomes a new project and they try to nurture them. This enables the man in their life to sit right back, put his feet up and enjoy the royal treatment. He learns to treat her as a passive individual and gets what he wants all the time but whenever she asks something of him, he is too busy.

These women have also affectionately been referred to as "saviors." Some would say they are getting what they deserve and what they ask for. The relationship is not one based on reciprocity. In fact, it is total giving on her part and total take on his part. However, she feels like it is her job to always give and he believes if she is willing to give, then he is going to take this free-ride as long as it lasts! This is not altruism on her part. She is not the incarnation of Mother Theresa.

True saviors are always trying to save someone out of the goodness of their heart. There is nothing wrong with this if this gives them extreme gratification and happiness. Unfortunately, women who choose men and establish these kinds of relationships grow unsatisfied with the passing of time. In fact, many start to wonder if they are truly appreciated by their mate. At some point, she begins to realize she is being taken advantage of and that she has chosen a turkey! The sad part is, when that relationship does end, she is likely to find herself in a similar one afterwards.

HOPEFUL DADDY WISHERS

In Illusion of Love, Celani discusses object relations and why women return to batterers or find repeated abusive relationships. Celani describes women who stay in abusive relationships as developing two selves; the hopeful self and the bused self. In the abused self, they take the abuse because their mate has them convinced that they deserve the abuse and after a while they believe it. In the hopeful self, they see their mate apologize for his abusive ways and promise to change. She hopes he really will change and she stays.

Celani and other psychoanalysts discuss how improper bonding with their fathers usually leads some women into finding negative relationships with men who are carbon copies of their fathers. Psychoanalysts believe these women unconsciously, or even consciously, select men who are like their fathers because it is their goal to be accepted by him. In selecting a man like their father, they unconsciously believe they can undo the rejection they experienced as a child if they can just get their mate to accept them!

I call women who choose men for this reason as "hopeful daddy wishers." These women are drawn to men who best represent their fathers. I am not saying the majority of fathers are bad, because they are not. Rather, it is women who were coddled too much by their fathers or not given any affection who seek out "father figures" in their relationships. These could be the types of women who are attracted to much older men who are well established and become "sugar daddies." Also, these could be women who have very little social or career skills, who have always been taken care of, or are afraid to endeavor into a career or venture out into the world. They go right from their parents' house to their husband's house, where she miserably lives and asks herself, "there must be more to life, no?"

If this is the type of relationship you desire and you are truly happy, then more power to you. For those women who are discontent with these types of relationships, you might have to take a look back at your childhood and do a self-evaluation. Do you choose men that best resemble your father because you are trying to replace or compensate for a relationship you did not have when you were younger? Do these relationships provide the chance for growth, healthy change, and happiness? If they don't, what are you going to do to try to bring peace of mind with your discontentment from the past?

MAN-EATER

Are you a woman who is fed up with most if not all men? Do you find that most of the men you meet play games and lead you on only to break your heart? Has it come to the point where you have developed an "I don't care" attitude and "I am going to break his heart for a change" mentality? Do you enter into relationships with this outlook only to find that it is your heart that keeps getting broken? If so, then perhaps you are what I would call a man-eater!

Some women get their hearts broken so many times that they become very angry, fed-up, and even numb to emotion. They vow never to fall in love again and if they are going to enter into a relationship, it will be her who breaks the man's heart! Often times, women with this attitude find themselves on the short end of the stick. It usually does not turn out as they hoped for. In fact, they find themselves falling in love with the man they wanted to abhor! Why does this happen?

Women who carry chips on their shoulders are most likely to radiate non-verbal cues which say "I'm angry, stay away" and "caution, danger, I will eat you alive." What sane man in the world wants to get involved with this type of woman? Most would probably pick up on the signs and turn and walk the other way. What type of man would be interested in the man-eater? Perhaps the one who likes a good challenge and views relationships as a game? Remember, in every relationship there is always a winner and a loser. Do you think he is going to play to lose? Heck no! By their very nature, men are very competitive. The game player views the man-eater as a tough nut to crack, but he will try. If he doesn't crack her, he will walk away and find another woman.

He woos her with his charm and says all the right things she needs to hear. He gradually wears her guard down by telling her all the things she needs to hear. She slowly lowers her resistance after a long battle with inner conflict and turmoil. She doesn't want to fall for him but finds herself starting to love him. As soon as she is willing to give her full love and attention to him, he bolts! Game over for her again and all she is left with is another broken heart. Can you blame her for being so bitter?

The man-eater needs time to regroup and collect her feelings. She needs to realize she is not a bad woman. She needs to see that her angry and hurt state attracts players who are likely to take advantage of her. Until she is able to forgive herself for making a bad choice in a man and forgive him for what he has done, she will remain vulnerable and likely attract another player.

SADSACK

Do you constantly wear your heart on your sleeve? Are you the type of woman who has always been walked all over by men? Do you ever really get to date men you dream of dating? Are you the type of woman who is always miserable in your relationships, always sad? Perhaps you are what I refer to as a sadsack!

I find that these types of women look for relationships more so than men. That's right, they are sad and need a relationship to make them happy. They believe in the poems, the songs, and the Hollywood movies which tell you that the only way you will ever find happiness is to find a man! So these women are always looking for that man who as one actor from a popular movie once phrased it "completes them."

Interestingly, women who are sadsacks are always sad with whoever they are with. When they are not in a relationship, they are sad because they are alone. When they are in a relationship, they are sad because of who they are with, or just unhappy with the relationship. They find that no one can really take their sadness away and they keep hoping for the "White Knight" to come and rescue them. In the meantime, they will remain sad" as they like to complain about their sadness to those who will listen.

I often wonder if these individuals have any conceptions of what happiness is. There are a lot of people in the world who have been depressed from the time they can remember. They either suffer from clinical depression or have been raised in an environment where feelings are suppressed and they have never been allowed to express their true feelings.

Happiness is a very relative term. It means many different things for everyone. When one enters into a relationship with the sole priority to be happy, they are fooling themselves as well as placing unrealistic expectations on their mate to try and keep them happy. Individuals have to assume responsibility for their own happiness, even if it means being alone for a time to take a personal inventory and seek out what is truly best for their lives. Jumping into a relationship with the hope of finding happiness will only lead to further disappointment and sadness.

Remember, no one can make you happy. You are responsible for your own happiness and a mate can only add to your happiness by accenting your life!

LOVERS OF RELATIONSHIPS

Are you the type of woman who is "in love" with the idea of being in love? Do you believe you have to be in love with someone to be happy? Lovers of relationships are very much like sadsacks but different because they usually are not as depressed. These types of individuals romanticize about being in love with someone. What is most important for them is not being in love with another individual, rather the relationship they are in.

For these individuals, the relationship usually starts out like "gang busters!" They are so "in love" with their new mate and can't wait to see them and be with them all the time. In fact, if they could get married right off the bat, many would.

It is not uncommon for them to be cohabitating with their new mate within a couple of weeks after meeting. They love the idea of living with someone and being in love with them. Unfortunately, these relationships seldom last because individuals fall out of love with the relationship just as fast and with their mate who they were never really in love with to begin with.

Lovers of relationships usually find themselves at two ends of the pivotal continuum: either bailing from one relationship to another, or trapped in a relationship they don't want to be in. For those bailing, they look to fall in love with a new relationship. They may engage in affairs to satiate their craving for a new relationship. They may leave their mate for another relationship since they were never truly in love to begin with. On the other hand, those who are in love with being in a relationship may become trapped. They might be too afraid to leave and hurt the person they have gotten involved with. They may choose to stay in the relationship because the relationship provides comfort, security, and a sense of safety even though they are very unhappy. And they might stay in the relationship because they believe the relationship is all they truly have.

I tend to find individuals suffering from personality disorders like: dependent personality disorder, borderline personality disorder, and some compulsive personality disorders fit this profile. If you are one who is a lover of relationships, it is time to learn how to separate individuals from the relationships they are in. You have to recognize that even though someone is inclusive in a relationship, they are also exclusive in which they have a separate identity. Most importantly, you have to see yourself as having a separate identity from the relationship. Learn to love someone for who they are rather than because they are a means to an end for establishing a relationship.

PASSIVE-AGGRESSIVE LOVERS

Do you find yourself seemingly involved in one relationship after another where you initiate or play games? Are you constantly using gaming ploys and tests to see how much your partner really cares for you? Does it seem you have a tendency to scare the men you really want to be with away from you? If so, perhaps you are a passive-aggressive lover!

Passive-aggressive lovers are those individuals who seem to always feel the need to test their partner's true affections, intentions, and commitment to relationships. Passive-aggressive people are often times ineffective communicators and are more likely to be manipulators of others. They do not really know how to get what they want from others so they are likely to use underhanded ways to test or control others.

These types of lovers are most likely to use game playing exercises without their partner's knowledge. They may simulate situations and events where they watch their partner perform and then question their actions. For example, you want to test your partner's undivided attention so you take him to a beach where there are many almost-naked women walking past both of you. You want to see if he watches or ogles any of them. Each time he glances at them, you crucify him and question his true devotion to you. You might also play other types of games like ignoring him when you don't get what you want, not answering his phone calls when something has not gone the way you planned, or over-reacting at very minor situations.

If you repetitiously act this way over a period of time, it is likely he will grow bored of your "histrionic" personality and will bail out of the relationship. No one likes to feel manipulated or put to the test, especially by those who we love.

Be careful yourself not to get hooked up with a passive-aggressive lover, who is always putting you to the test. At what limit will it end? They will often explain it away as, "I did it because I love you or wanted to see how much you love me." Remember, true love is unconditional and should not be based on manipulated trials and tribulations because there are enough of those which occur naturally. If you sense your love is part of some "science experiment", it would be a good time for you to say "thanks for coming out" and leave!

PASSIVE LOVERS

Are you always the one who gives and gives but never gets anything in return in a relationship? Do you find you are contributing in a major way to this problem because you are afraid to speak up and say what you really want to say?

Most of all, do you feel that your rights and freedoms are being taken away? If so, you are a passive lover!

Passive lovers are those much like Florence nightingales, who are willing to let others run their lives. Often times, they say and do the opposite of what they really want and this leads to extreme feelings of stress and frustration for both partners. Your mate asks you to go somewhere but you had other plans and you would rather do your own thing. Instead of declining his offer, you say, "yes, I will go" when you would have rather said, "no, I have made other plans." In saying yes to his offer, which was made without him knowing you had other plans, you sit and stew all night. He asks you what's wrong and you reply "nothing!" In fact, it gets to the point where you get mad at him whenever he asks you to do anything because you know you won't be able to turn him down and this annoys you.

Why do you say "yes" when you really mean "no"? Is it because you believe if you turn him down it will hurt his feelings and you don't want to make him upset? So instead, you make yourself upset and leave him guessing at your mood swings! At some point, he will be afraid to ask you to do anything because he just doesn't understand where you are coming from.

Most passive lovers have become this way due to their upbringing. They were usually raised in a family setting where there was a very domineering parent (or parents) who basically taught children not to express emotions and to "be seen and not heard." If children spoke up, they were reprimanded or belittled to the point of feeling rejected. As adults, individuals do not want to be rejected by their mates so they "go along" with their mate's every wish even though it makes them miserable.

Relationships of this nature usually crumble because one or both of them begin to develop an intolerance for the other as time passes. The passive lover begins to resent their mate for always asking them to do things and placing them in a situation they would rather not be in even though they do not know how to say "no." These lovers' mates develop an impatience for their inability to think for themselves and may even begin to disrespect them. Unfortunately, many times this disrespect may spill into manipulation, verbal or physical abuse because they know they can get away with it and their lover is too afraid to speak up. Usually, no one feels very good in this type of relationship. Passive lovers truly do not feel respected and most have no one to blame but themselves for not speaking up!

ASSERTIVE LOVERS

Assertive lovers are those who are very well-balanced in most areas of their lives. They are lovers who know what they want in a relationship and how to get what they want. What is most important is that they get what they want but also respect the rights of their mate. They view relationships as both accentuated and reciprocal.

When you view a relationship as accentuated, you recognize the need to maintain your own identity and remain who you always were. You don't compromise yourself into becoming someone you are not. You also do not let your mate run your life and you don't sell your soul to him to be loved and accepted. Even though the two of you are an item, you still both maintain your distinct identities and personalities. You view a relationship as one where your mate compliments who you are and what you want in a relationship, rather than complicating your life!

A reciprocal relationship is one where there is equal give and take. When I say "equal" I am referring to all aspects; emotional, physical, psychological, social, and spiritual. There will be something you are more proficient at, and there will be other things he is more proficient at. The two of you work to establish a common bond and harmony in the relationship. You truly do accent each other in most aspects of your relationship.

These types of lovers are able to maintain the best relationships because they are honest and forthright. Both partners feel good about themselves, about each other and about the relationship. It is a good relationship because assertive lovers view their mates as their best friends and share their feelings, ideas, beliefs, and dreams with them. They establish a deep level of intimacy in their relationship which creates a solid bond. They are honest with their mates and they expect the same in return. Bottom line...They settle for no one less than who they are!

There are probably many other types of lovers who are a culmination of the ones mentioned. Keep in mind, both women and men are capable of being any of the types of lovers I listed. After all is said and done, you are the one who has to love and be in the relationship. It is up to you to decide who you want and what type of relationship you want. The majority of relationships will be determined by who you are at that given point in your life. You will select mates based on your level of maturity of self as well as your perception of how relationships should be. Conversely, others with similar backgrounds will be drawn to you and may also seek you out.

You always have the final say in what type of relationship you choose to enter and what type of lover you want to get involved with. However, to better understand others who you might choose to get involved with, you first have to develop a better understanding of "self". Be selective, know yourself and give yourself time between relationships!

CHAPTER FIFTEEN

KNOW WHAT YOU REALLY WANT

Love is the great miracle cure. Loving ourselves works miracles in our lives.

Louise Hay

Everybody has some general idea of who their desirable mate should be like. Why do we settle for someone who is less than desirable? Do women actively seek men who they know will not make ideal partners? What can you do for yourself when it comes to selecting your ideal mate?

Don't settle for someone who does not meet your expectations or desires! Spend your time with people you are most happy to be around. Make sure you are happy with yourself instead of looking for ways for your partner to make you happy. Furthermore, choose a mate who you feel compatible with and is a reciprocal in their affection. Life is too short for charades and games. There is no such thing as a "perfect person", but there is someone out there who is a perfect fit for you.

In the courses and seminars in relationships and communication I teach, I am often times asked by women what they can do differently to make their current or next relationship grow and flourish. I try not to sound too "preachy" but I offer four pieces of advice which might make things more productive, but don't guarantee eternal happiness or bliss.

1) WAIT TIL YOU ARE THIRTY!

The average age that people are getting married by had increased two years since 1980. Women tend to marry at 24 years and men marry at 27 years of age. Those getting married younger are usually well into their second or third marriages by the time they are 30. The reason I am saying to wait until you are 30 years old, or close to it, is because by then you have a better understanding of what you want in life and where you are going. Too many people get married too young and realize they don't want to start a family, rather they want to go back to school or move away to pursue their careers. Also, many individuals are still finding out who they are in their twenties. They are not too far removed from their teenage years where they were just learning the many responsibilities of life. The twenties should be a time for you to practice and explore life and live out your own personal responsibilities.

Some people are not mature enough to be with only one person. There are those still sowing their "wild oats" and they are still kids in the candy store. It seems by 30 years of age, most get the wild partying ways out of our systems and something clicks inside of us and says, "what are you going to do with your life?" Try to wait until you are thirty. Know yourself and what you want in life.

2) DATE... DON'T MATE!

Be selective about who you start your relationships with. Many relationships evolve into marriages because of unplanned pregnancies. Women sometimes get trapped because of an accident. Whenever you have sex with someone there is always the chance of pregnancy. Ask yourself, "Do I know this person well enough and love them enough to be the father of my child?" Interestingly, women coming out of failed marriages based on unexpected pregnancies assert their child is the best and only thing to come from the marriage, but if they could do it all over again their husband would have never been their mate or father of their child.

Some women fall in love at first sight and jump in way too deep. People fall in love with the idea of being "in love" and some are led with their emotions and not their heads. Too many people live in common-law marriages. Those living together before marriage are more likely to get divorced. There are more pressures and expectations put on them by society, family, friends, and themselves.

Date and see who and what is out there. Be comfortable with yourself and date people who are positive, mentally stable, goal oriented, and happy with who they are.

3) SAY NO TO ALL ABUSE!

No man ever has the right to abuse a woman! No woman ever has to take abuse from a man. The general rule of thumb is if he abuses you before you're married, he's going to do it when you are married. You owe it to yourself and your children to not to stay in situations which are not conducive to mental and physical health. Each time he abuses you and you stay, it does two things. One, it tells him he can keep doing it and get away with it. Two, it robs you of your self-esteem and leads you to feeling weak and helpless.

If every woman said no to abuse, men would have no one to abuse but themselves. Just say no! In doing so, you are sending men the message they need to take a long look at themselves and get help in order to truly change.

4) STICK TO YOUR GUNS!

When you make decisions about anything, learn to feel good about them. Remember, if you can't make yourself happy, then no one else will. In psychology there is an equation called the Equity Theory (Walster, Walster, & Berscheid, 1978; Messick & Cook, 1983). This theory claims you should develop and maintain relationships in which the ratio of your rewards compared to costs is approximately equal to your partners. What does this mean? What you put into the relationship, you get back! If you are a communicator and need to discuss an issue, then you are opening

yourself up and giving to your partner. Make sure your partner reciprocates the action. Make your relationships correspond where you feel
it is equally give and take.

CASE STUDY

Robert and Beth have been married for 8 years now. They have a very good marriage. The key to their marriage is communication. They are sure to always keep the lines of communication open at all costs. They sit down each day and try to make time for discussion and for the children. While other marriages have failed around them, their marriage continues to stay strong. Both believe their spouse is their best friend and they can say anything to them. Beth claims the key to their happiness is their unconditional love for one another. She points out they have their moments of disagreement and arguments but she says the most important thing they share is the desire to resolve issues together. In the beginning, Robert thought he was incapable of being a father, or even a husband for that matter, because it meant a big time responsibility. Moreover, it meant that he had to change! The idea of this kind of change was very frightening to him. He loved Beth too much to not be with her. He was content being a bachelor, but he did want to get married and believed all relationships involve taking chances and work. He took the plunge and has no regrets. In fact, Robert says the best thing about his marriage is growing with Beth and the kids. Each year, they take a family trip to somewhere new. And each year, Robert and Beth also attend a weekend marriage retreat to get to know one another. Beth also asserts that one of the strongest binding ties is their belief in God and their commitment to living a good, clean lifestyle. She smiles and says, "by taking vows, I remember hearing, let no man break apart what God has brought together."

• Marriage is a life-long commitment for you, your mate, and your children. It is an awesome commitment filled with a great many rewards!

CHAPTER SIXTEEN

HOW WILL I KNOW WHO IS RIGHT FOR ME?

We come to love not by finding a perfect person, but by learning to see an imperfect person perfectly.

Anonymous

Who is Mr. Right? What does he look like? What does he act like? What kind of career should he be endeavoring in? And what are the physical and psychological characteristics of a Miss Right? Given that men and women differ in their perceptions of how they perceive one another, do you think their "mark" for the "perfect mate" is going to be more accurate?

Often times I am asked where one finds their ideal mate. Shouldn't it be the same like shopping for a house or a car? You don't want to get stuck with a lemon, right? I would never go so far as to characterize or classify people as chattel or superficial objects such as houses or cars. Interestingly, some individuals get so fed up with repeated failed relationships that they adopt the same attitude as they would when shopping for appliances.

Well then, what should one look for in a mate? Perhaps the best answer to that question is to make a personal inventory of yourself and work forward in a progressive manner. Remember, we tend to attract others or gravitate toward those who are much like ourselves. If you keep attracting individuals who you don't like, or find that they bring trouble into your life, perhaps there is a certain aspect of yourself which you need to address.

As human beings, we struggle with the task of looking within ourselves to see what makes us tick. Moreover, when faced with the opportunity to correct some inadequacy within ourselves, most choose to avoid dealing with purging the soul and mind of past issues. Why is that? Well, for some the process is too painful. Unfortunately, most of the pain that haunts us can be traced back to early childhood where we experienced it in our interactions with our parents and loved ones. Some of these hurts actually represent the only connections individuals had with parents and loved ones, regardless of how dysfunctional and destructive they were! When individuals are led on an introspective journey by therapists or other helping professionals, they uncover these deep, dark pains which continually perpetuate dysfunction in their adult lives. You can see how painful this might be, even with the help of a therapist. Therefore, many individuals continue to carry with them "baggage" from one relationship to the next, where other individuals might be carrying just as much baggage or more! Keep in mind that you always take with you something from every relationship you are in. If you have more inadequate relationships than good ones, less than desirable memories and qualities may stick with you. You start your own collection of suffering. It is like a huge magnet picking up scrap in a wrecking yard. How do you resolve this? Turn off the magnet!

What I mean by turning off the magnet is to prevent negativity from grabbing hold of you. People can be negative and you need to avoid allowing negative people to influence you. When lecturing, I often refer to extremely negative people as "psychical vampires." If you are a positive person or relatively middle of the road with your moods, when these people are around you, you begin to feel drained because they zap energy from you. They are negative people who consciously or unconsciously try to bring you down. You need to avoid them!

Before you can be happy in any relationship, you first have to learn to be happy with yourself! For many, being alone is a very scary prospect. Perhaps it has a lot to do with societal values and messages which teach us that being alone is the same as being a loser. If you are alone, then that must mean no one loves you or values your company enough to be with you and that must make you a loser. Translated, you must be so inadequate that no one wants to be around you. That is a scary rationalization but many people hold it as their gospel truth. "It's better to be miserable and in a relationship for all the wrong reasons, than to just be alone!" This couldn't be farther from the truth. A relationship should be based on happiness, contentment, joy, compatibility, and reciprocity. Good relationships do not thrive on misery. In fact, they become more dysfunctional and lead people into developing irrational thought patterns.

When irrational thought patterns begin to develop in one's perception of relationships, not only are they likely to botch things in relationships they are in, but also choose partners who are "perfect" matches for their irrational thought patterns. Unfortunately, most people with these irrational thought patterns do not take the time to re-evaluate themselves when a relationship ends. Many feel the need to jump into a new relationship immediately. Some are afraid to look within themselves, introspect and see what needs changing. It takes work and most people just do not have the time or want to make the time!

Who is your ideal mate? The best way to answer that question is to ask yourself, "Who Am I?" Whenever I conduct workshops, lectures, or see clients and they ask me about their "ideal mate", I quickly turn it back on them and ask them about themselves. Who are you? I ask that question in the present tense. You see, it is very important for people to view things in the present because you don't want them listing qualities of their "ideal self", what they someday want to be. Very much like their "ideal mate", someone who they will someday want to meet.

You need to know who you are right now. Once you figured out who you are , you can then work from that point onward. You can change things within yourself, focusing on strengths and areas needing improvement.

The most important part of this exercise is to become aware of you. For some, this is going to be an introduction of sorts.

In the fields of holistic medicine and health, you often times come across a a system which looks at biology, psychology, and sociology combined. It is often times referred to as a bio-psycho-socio model. Rather than there being only one influence in a person's life, there is a combination of three. In my practice, I like to add a fourth component, spiritualism. And when I refer to spiritualism, I am referring to one's faith and religiosity. For some cultures and religions, having the same faith is essential for making a marriage work.

I like to have client's create a page and list the four components as such:

ATTRIBUTE	STRENGTHS	WEAKNESSES
PHYSICAL HEALTH		
MENTAL HEALTH		
SPIRITUAL LIFE		
SOCIAL LIFE		

At first glance, the assignment looks rather simplistic and very general. I ask clients to sub-divide the four categories into sub-types where they will look at others areas within each to see influences on their lives. The following sub-categories I like to use are the following:

PHYSICAL HEALTH
- eating habits
- exercise
- hygiene
- satisfaction with body
- overall physical health
- rest/sleep
- use of alcohol/drugs

MENTAL HEALTH
- self-esteem
- stable moods
- positive attitude/outlook
- takes responsibility for feelings
- generally content
- goal oriented
- continually evolving
- open-minded
- can trust others
- loves to laugh/humor
- manages stress
- happy with self

SPIRITUAL

- believes in God or a Divine being
- attends church or services
- is reverent of all life
- respects other's religious choices
- believes in raising children in a religious household
- enjoys praying

SOCIAL LIFE

- has friends
- has family
- likes the company of others
- likes own company
- has and chooses reliable friends
- stays away from negative people
- doesn't conform to other's ideals
- has someone close to disclose to
- value open communication
- makes time for those in your life
- leaves abusers/abusive situations
- doesn't need alcohol or drugs to be social

As you can see the sub-categories go into a little more depth However, this exercise is by no means meant to be a psychological test. I like to refer to it as a personal inventory. By going through each category, people learn more about themselves; what motivates them and the type of person they are. Basically, it is a "Who Am I" inventory. It tells you who you are.

Once you have figured out who you are, you then can think about what you want in a mate. Instead of settling, you can be actively selective in finding someone who is like you...like you now!

Here is a sample of a "marriage-attitude" inventory you might find interesting. There are *reflection* questions. Throughout my years of counseling and research, several key issues have come to the forefront regarding couples. I have taken some of the most poignant issues and put them into questions to consider about your spouse. This is a good way not only to learn about your mate or potential mate but also about yourself and how you look at relationships. I offer clients and students these questions to ponder and discuss:

1) I expect my mate to complete me and make me happy. A sense of true happiness and completion comes from love and marriage, so I was taught to believe:

True
False

2) My partner should know my needs, desires, and ambitions without me having to tell them because we've been together long enough:

True
False

3) I expect my mate to like my family and friends. They should if they truly love me. They are a part of the package deal:

True
False

4) Men and women are very different. My partner should have the same ideologies about gender roles, gender identities, and expectations as myself:

True
False

5) Family, religion, and politics are very important to me. My partner should have the same beliefs as me or at least convert over for me:

True
False

6) My partner and I should have the same sexual needs and attitudes. If we differ, they should always strive to please me:

True
False

7) My partner should stay the same way emotionally as they were in the beginning when we

met. They should not change in any way, which will hinder or hurt our relationship. We should strive to evolve together at the same time when change is necessary:

True
False

8) I believe communication is the key ingredient to any lasting relationship. A relationship will fail if we stop communicating. I feel it is my duty to always initiate discussions:

True
False

9) All arguments, conflict, and confrontation should be avoided in a relationship. There is no need to argue:

True
False

10) I believe marriage should be a onetime deal for me and I intend on staying married to the same individual for better or for worse, especially for the children, even if there is abuse. No matter what happens in my marriage, I am in it for life:

True
False

11) I believe there is a place for abuse in relationships. All relationships have some component of abuse:

True
False

12) It's easy to get a divorce today and the majority of marriages wind up there anyway. Knowing this, I can go into any marriage hoping for the best but expecting the worst:

True
False

13) Cheating in a marriage is okay as long as you don't get caught:

True
False

14) Cyber sex is okay to engage in. It is not really cheating:

True
False

15) Pornography is a good thing to watch. I can fulfill my fantasies, which my partner can't or won't:

True
False

16) Self-administered surveys in magazines are a great place to figure out how compatible you are with your mate:

True
False

17) I believe relationships are highly over-rated and the idea of finding a perfect soul mate is an illusion, sometimes you just have to settle:

True
False

18) I hold onto "emotional baggage" from previous relationships, which hinder my current relationships:

True
False

19) I am afraid of loving someone because I fear getting hurt again:

    True
    False

20) I believe that sometimes turning to a counselor or outside help is needed to save a relationship:

    True
    False

The purpose of this inventory is not intended for you to carry it around with you and hand it to prospective mates to fill out! Nor was it intended to give to your current partner to see how compatible you are. In fact, it is designed more for you. It is a guide to help you examine who you are and what your attitudes are about marriage. You can't change another person, but you can change the way you look at things.

If you believe that marriage is like having a baby or caring for a pet, that it is a "pet project" for you to care for, to nurture and mold into the image you want, then your outlook on marriage and the person you plan on marrying is definitely jaded. Some people need to be happily married to themselves before they can marry someone else, and the "baggage" and quirks they will bring to the relationship.

QUIZ RESULTS:

For those curious to see how you scored on the quiz or what it meant, based on the years of doing counseling, research and interviewing experts in the field, scoring "true" for questions 1-19 demonstrate aspects of rigid thinking, non-compromise, authoritarian beliefs for relationships as well as truly believing that your partner be perfect or as close to perfect-- "the perfect partner"! If you answered "true" for question #20, then you realize that sometimes help in a relationship is required from the outside.

If you answered "TRUE" for any of the following questions: 1-8, 10, 11, 17 & 18 then you are operating on a belief system that fosters many of the characteristics of co-dependency. I strongly recommend checking out any of the following websites which explain the aspects of co-dependent behavior:

http://www.allaboutcounseling.com/codependency.htm
http://www.recovery-man.com/coda/codependency.htm

http://www.addictionz.com/codependency.htm

If you answered "TRUE" for questions: 9, 12-16 & 19, you may possess aspects seen in co-dependent relationships that are more avoidant in nature or possess aspects of Independent Personality Disorder/Avoidant Personality Disorder. Please visit the following websites to learn more:

http://www.webmd.com/anxiety-panic/guide/dependent-personality-disorder

http://psychcentral.com/disorders/sx8.htm

http://www.nlm.nih.gov/medlineplus/ency/article/000940.htm

CHAPTER SEVENTEEN

ABUSE TOUCHES ALL WALKS OF LIFE!

'Tis better to have loved and lost...Than never to have loved at all.

Alfred, Lord Tennyson, **In Memoriam,**

It has been said that the greatest illusion the Devil created was to convince people he wasn't real. If you don't believe it, if you don't see it, then it can't be real—right? The same can be said for upscale and upper class marriages. There was a time when you didn't hear about abuse in those "types" of marriages, as it was believed money was the true root of all happiness—right? Wrong! News reports, studies, and self-help authors report abuse, neglect, and dissatisfaction in all types of marriage regardless of class status, religion or skin color. Bad things really do happen to good people and rich people. And they don't have to if you don't let them!

The O.J. Simpson trial in the United States of America back in the 1990's was an eye-opener for people who believed rocks were never chucked in glass houses, namely those of the rich and famous. During the Simpson trials, where the former NFL star was tried for the murders of his ex-wife Nicole Brown Simpson and her companion Ron Goldman, the public was made privy to 911 calls Nicole had made in the past reporting instances of abuse she had received from O.J. Ironically, these tapes were only truly taken seriously after she was found dead, body severely hacked to pieces on the sidewalk. It was then that the public released an outcry as to why nothing was done to O.J. when she first started reporting the abuse (McDermott,1995). For those not familiar with the Simpson case, O.J. was found not guilty in either of the deaths he was accused of committing. Furthermore, in the USA, one has the right to try someone civilly for "wrongful deaths." Simpson was tried in this forum by the Goldman family. In the end, Simpson was liable for the 1994 death of Goldman and committed battery against his ex-wife Nicole. A civil trial jury came to this precarious ruling on February 4, 1997.

I am not here to preach about or castigate the short-comings in the U.S. judicial system, even though it would appear to be flawed according to many as far as justice being truly served. That is not my bone of contention. Conversely, I want to applaud the judicial system for allowing the 911 Nicole Brown Simpson tapes to be heard by all. It was about time the public was served a harsh wake-up call to the realities of the rich and famous, tinsel town, and other referent power holders. The message came through loud and clear! No matter how much money one has, it doesn't make them the perfect spouse. No matter how many movies or Academy Awards someone has won, it doesn't make them the perfect spouse. No matter how many trophies or championships one has achieved, it doesn't make them infallible. No matter how good looking or charismatic one is, or if they've been on the cover of People magazine, Sports Illustrated, TV Guide or GQ. It doesn't make them the perfect spouse. And it doesn't matter what religious denomination one belongs to, it doesn't make them infallible or perfect!

All abuse is wrong! No one should ever have to live in fear or hurt. I am glad that a positive came out of a very negative situation. The public at large could now see with their own eyes that this kind of abuse happens in the "best of homes." For those who were victims of abuse, believing in the excuses that "it's finances", "it's lack of resources", "it's lack of education", or "it's the alcohol and drugs that make him/her violent" could now see that anyone could be a victim of domestic abuse. Abuse and neglect know no boundaries and don't discriminate.

As former Editor-in-chief of Vices: The Magazine for Addictions, Habits and Well-Being, I have learned all too well from the misconceptions many people have when it comes to addictions, mental health, and happiness. We have an interactive website and see how so many people are naïve and oblivious to addiction, addictive personalities, and abuse. Our mission statement/motto is *ADDICTIONS DON'T DISCRIMINATE; PEOPLE DO!* I think the same can be said of abusive and neglectful relationships, whether you are talking about spousal abuse, child abuse, or even senior abuse. *ABUSE DOESN'T DISCRIMINATE EITHER!*

It's funny to think about how reality television has made people's lives in Hollywood, the music world or entertainment appear to put a spin on art imitating life and life imitating art. There is not one week, let alone a day, which passes by where you turn on some Entertainment Tonight show and see the latest actor/actress, musician, artist, athlete, or politician getting arrested, going into detox, or suffering from some another kind of tragedy. It would seem today's society revolves around "reality television." This type of television brings the "real lives" of celebrities into your living rooms and family rooms. The viewing public is interested in watching celebrity train wrecks. It would appear some TV viewers take some morbid pleasure or comfort in seeing that the "upper echelon" of society is more screwed up than they are! It's like driving on the highway, seeing an accident and just having to slow down and take a look. Television and rag tabloids bring you these accidents and train wrecks so you, too, can see how you and your relationships measure up!

Over the years I've seen women from upscale marriages who were abused-turned authors appearing on TV talk shows to share their harrowing stories and words of wisdom to women currently in abusive relationships. Their words ring clear to women who are being abused by their mates. It all sounds the same. In fact, it sounds like the same movie being played over and over, but this time the cast of characters being played by different people. It's very real in all marriages, regardless of socio-economic status.

I had a chance to sit down and chat with two very different women who literally came from different sides of the proverbial train tracks. Marta is a woman who is married to a very wealthy entrepreneur. Vicki is a former prostitute. Both had very profound things to share with me. In order to make things easier to follow, I thought it would be easiest to include the interviews in their original formats.

Even though people know the whys, it's what they do next which matters most. It really becomes a matter of life and death for some women! Marta's words speak of how appearances can be deceiving:

PAS: How real is abuse in rich and upscale marriages?

MARTA: "Most people are oblivious that this kind of stuff really happens to people with lots of money, or who are rich. Abuse affects all walks of life. Trust me, rocks are thrown in glass houses. *(pausing)* I have the broken windows to prove it!"

PAS: What prompted you to leave your marriage after years of abuse?

MARTA: *(Deep breath)* "After 22 years of being with a rich and powerful man, who had people eating out of his hands; lawyers, cohorts, accountants, politicians, other people's wives, ministers, it was time to wake up.

People are naïve to think it doesn't happen to rich people. Often times, we associate fame, fortune, and power with the fairy tale, happily-ever-after scenario and that is not the case! I hid the abuse for as long as I could. My daughter, who went away to private school begged me to leave her father. As much as she loves her father, she knew well enough that what he was doing to me was wrong. It was only after my son suggested that what my husband was doing to me was wrong and that I was in essence condoning the behavior and encouraging him to follow in his father's footsteps did the wakeup call slap me across the face. It's funny, but his slaps and punches were never as bad as this one. This was sobering!"

PAS: Do you think people can become addicted to abuse?

MARTA: "Interesting question...I think over a period of time, you just get used to it and grow numb. The pattern grows stale for both and you literally play out a damaging situation and don't even know how the heck it even started. For me, I was addicted to the abuse, rather the pattern...conditioned to it. *(reflection)* What I did become addicted to was booze and some drugs. When I went through detox and treatment, I must say it was another wake up call. I think if I didn't go into detox I would never have had the light bulb not only go on, but stay on. What my son and daughter were telling me made total sense."

PAS" What were you afraid of most?

MARTA: "Another interesting question. *(smile)* Funny, but I was never afraid of the abuse. I was most afraid when he wasn't abusing me. It made me wonder if there was someone else he was interested in and sleeping with. I was most afraid of being unattractive and unwanted. There were times when I was very afraid of losing my kids, my family, my self-respect...my husband, but after a while you grow detached from yourself and it leads you to being afraid of nothing. I take that back...It makes you afraid of not knowing the difference."

PAS: What difference is that?

MARTA: "Actually, knowing whether you are still alive or already dead."

PAS: What do you mean by that?

MARTA: You become so numb and so detached. Not only at an emotional level, but at physical and spiritual levels as well. I was drinking to try and feel something...anything. When he hit me or when I woke up the next day hung over, feeling sick and hurting were the signs pointing to life...I could still feel, therefore I must be alive."

PAS: Does someone who stays in an abusive relationship act as an enabler to abuse? You said your son posed this to you. Do you buy into it?

MARTA: "After a while you start to think you did something wrong and deserve the abuse. You really start to believe what you are doing or have done warrants what is dished out your way. I am a person who believes in karma. What goes around comes around and I must have done something to deserve this wrath. Looking back, I would definitely have to say hindsight is 20/20 and yes, I enabled it to a degree because I was an active participant in the situation. If I would have said no at any point, especially right from the get-go, and walked away, who would he have had to abuse, right?"

PAS: Don't you think you are being too hard on yourself for thinking that way?

MARTA: "Absolutely not! As a matter of fact, if I would have had a backbone and been harder on myself, I wouldn't have wasted some of the best years of my life."

PAS: Do you believe that we all have choices when it comes to staying in a bad relationship, or do you become trapped?

MARTA: *(long sigh)* "Definitely you have choices! Even though you are numb, mentally and emotionally bent, screwed up, or whatever you want to call it, there are always signs, people along the way telling you what's going on is wrong. I knew it was wrong. I felt it was wrong. But you know what? It just was."

PAS: What type of woman gets abused or decides to stay in an upper class/wealthy marriage?

MARTA: "First off, I consider myself intelligent and successful in my own right. I finished college and had my own career started before meeting my husband. Saying that, I think any woman, whether rich or poor, stays for pretty much the same reasons...low self-esteem. It gets to a point where you not only blame yourself, but you also start to make excuses for your abusive spouse. When you get past that, there is also the issue of embarrassment and respect. You don't dare whine about it publicly or point fingers because you don't want to demean yourself further, or have others looking into your dirty laundry. You really feel ashamed that others will put you down and blame you for the marital problems. If your husband is well-liked, a standout in the community, then who will believe he could be abusive and the problem, right? You really feel like the lesser of the two and feel helpless. Who is going to believe me? You really worry about bringing shame and embarrassment to your family. You keep your mouth shut and try to minimize the damage."

PAS: Do you think it is likely the reverse happens?

MARTA: How so?

PAS: I have been a psychotherapist and professor for many years and hear about husbands being abuse by their wives. Do you think this happens just as much?

MARTA: "Absolutely! When I was working my meetings and participating in co-dependency therapy groups, we had men who were on the receiving end of abuse by their wives. This was definitely a real thing. And like myself, it wasn't people coming from low income housing projects who were the culprits and the victims. We're talking wealthy men being abused by wealthy wives! Not all the situations were based on physical abuse, rather it was more psychological and emotional in nature."

PAS: Psychological? How so?

MARTA: "From listening to these men, wives would hold things over their heads. Perhaps they had made mistakes at work or in their personal lives. Wives threatened to go public or tell significant others about these details. They would put their husbands in a state of duress or coercion to have them do things for them. In fact, some wives even threatened to turn the children against them, or take off with the children. And of course, some wives beat on their husbands, but these husbands were too embarrassed to cry out for help because they felt no one would believe them, or take them seriously. Furthermore, they felt that they risked losing their status and significant others if it was found out how weak they were."

PAS: You eluded to developing alcoholism and drug abuse. Was this a by-product of dealing with your dysfunctional marriage?

MARTA: *(short pause)* "Yes. I drank to numb the pain. Drinking and drugging was symptomatic of the abuse. I was indulging in other vices like gambling, shopping, and compulsive eating as a way to self-medicate myself. I even thought if I gained a lot of weight and kept myself unattractive, he would leave me alone. This didn't work. I did find that if I was wasted, he would leave me alone. I am guessing he thought I wasn't worth the trouble when I was in that state."

PAS: Would you say it is better to stay in the marriage for all of the wrong reasons then be alone for all of the right reasons? Does reasoning this way really support this notion?

MARTA: *(sigh)* "Yes, I was one of them. No one wants to be alone or rejected. We're human beings who crave love and acceptance. Sometimes, any amount of love combined with abuse is better than nothing for some. I bought into that notion. Is it right...no! Is it the right thing to stay...no! Is it wrong? No! Given what you know, think, and feel while you're in that period of your life, you do the best you can. At that moment, you are doing what you think is right for yourself with the mental and emotional tools you have. I realize I may be contradicting myself here, but what you are in I guess is a 'damned if you do, damned if you don't situation.' No matter how you cut it, on paper and in reality, all abuse is wrong."

PAS: Where are you today in your life?

MARTA: "I am single, I am happier, and working on myself. *(smiling)* I have forged ahead to re-establish relationships with my children, family, and friends. When you are in a bad situation, you isolate yourself to hide the pain and shame. Also, the abuser cuts you off from your lifelines. I am in the process of trying to re-attach severed ties. It is an on-going process, but I find the greatest severed tie I am working on is the connection to myself. I am working my groups and doing the therapy thing. I was once at a seminar you, Dr. Peter, put on. You discussed the notion of sweet acceptance versus bitter resistance when it comes to the only way of overcoming addiction. You said bitterness only perpetuates resistance to healing and change. I was there. I hated that place. Acceptance brings a feeling or refreshing...sweetness to one's life. Let's just say I am sweetening my bitter cup of coffee. Things are not as bitter and black as they once were. Life is starting to taste sweet again!"

In today's society, many women are still captivated by the lure of the "knight in shining armor" or the image of the "bad boy." What is it that makes these men so appealing? I have provided you in previous chapters with types of lovers I looked at why women are drawn to them. Did the media still exert this much control over us in 2008? Famous and popular movies like Jerry McGuire and Pretty Woman would dictate too many misinformed that you need someone else to "complete you" or "rescue you." Given the amount of dysfunction in Hollywood and other famous celebrities/athletes who are constantly getting into trouble with the law or who are in and out of rehab, it would appear many rich and famous people need their own keepers. And many of today's children, youth, and teens look up to these icons as their inspiration. What can we truly expect in generations to come—more dysfunction?

Over the last couple of years, some striking things have caught my attention. I spoke with a friend of mine, Academy Award winner, Joe Mayer, who also worked on the box office smash movie in the 1990's *Pretty Woman*. "The problem with Hollywood and the movie industry is more good, positive, inspirational movies are needed," according to Joe. People need hope! Viewers need positive role models they can relate to.

"One of the best movies I have seen in years is *March of the Penguins*," says Mayer. "This movie offers something for every viewer and it teaches great values. Hollywood needs more of these types of movies. We need to go back in time to an era where movies left something to the viewer, while at the same time entertaining and leaving a positive message."

Movies and media need icons that people can relate to in a positive way, offer the message of self-empowerment and, above all else, recognize the uniqueness of the individual. I remember driving home from a lecture a couple of years ago and listening to a poll a major radio station was holding for women listeners. The question polled was, "Who do you consider to be the sexiest man on television?" This was a large radio station with a listener base of well over 5 million people.

Obviously, the people who responded to this were mostly women. Did you know the majority picked a lying, womanizing, cheat murderer as "the most sexiest man" on television? You might know him as Tony Soprano from the Sopranos!

I remember the female DJ adding her own two cents about how sexy Soprano's character is, but she quickly added he cheated on his wife and loved to murder. To paraphrase her words, they went something like this... "As women, what kind of world do we live in today when we consider these attributes sexy in a man?" I couldn't have agreed more! You don't see too many men lusting after women who cheat and murder, and crown them great catches.

There are still too many women in today's world who look at men as referent power holders. They look to men to hold all of the power, make all of the big decisions, own all the money, and run their lives. The famous Marlboro cigarette ad from the 1970's poked fun at women who smoked as, "You've come a long way, baby." This was their sublime message for letting women know that just because they smoke like men, they are equal. It's funny, but referring to women as "baby" kind of undermines the whole notion of equality.

This is 2008 and we've all come a long way. People need to realize regardless of their gender, skin color, or religion that they are all equal. No one is more than or less than anyone else. We are all perfect in our own right.

A few years ago I was speaking with Jack Canfield, best known for the Chicken Soup for the Soul book series and the bestselling book, The Secret. I asked Jack a poignant question geared toward the notion of "self-help." I asked him, "Is there a point in addictions where self-help really becomes self-help?" Jack's response was what I expected and how people should view their lives---"Most people are dependent on each other in this life. We are interdependent. Interdependent is helpful, whereas codependency is not useful. When people move through self-help, you do for yourself what you have been demanding the environment to do for you. Expectations of the world often times create your own upsets. You see this in addictions to substances like heroin, etc. We become more self-sufficient over time when we are able to be at peace with ourselves."

A few years ago, a team I put together filmed a documentary series entitled, Criminal Minds: Criminal Intent. The show examined the motives as to why criminals commit or participate in certain types of crimes. The first episode we shot examined prostitution. During the filming, I was able to chat with Vicki, a former prostitute who was leaving the mean streets of her trade after engaging in the sex industry for nearly 15 years.

This is what Vicki had to say about life on the streets working as a prostitute:

PAS: Please don't take this as an insult, but you look very weathered and beaten.

VICKI: "That's what working the streets will do to you. That's what taking drugs and smack will turn you into…"

PAS: You say you've worked on the streets for 15 years. Why?

VICKI: "The bottom line is always the cash. You start out to make money to try to make a life for yourself. You stay in it to support your death."

PAS: Support your death?

VICKI: "Yeah…being a junkie. As far as I am concerned, once you're hooked on meth, crack, and heroin, you're a walking dead person, like in the monster movies. This shit helps the brain cells…if there are any left."

PAS: So you got into hooking because of the money? And why this line of work when you could make money at other things?

VICKI: "Easy cash. You don't actually have to get up early every day and be on the same schedule. And hey, its sex…doesn't sex feel good and you get paid for it right?"

PAS: After doing it as long as you have, was it worth it…the money and all?

VICKI: *(long pause)* "If I had to do it again...no. Was it worth it? You make do with what you got. I didn't think I had a lot of options when I was a kid going on the streets. Looking back, yeah, there were other options and I guess I was a dumb ass punk who thought they knew it all. When you're a kid a hundred bucks for a couple of hours work looks like a lot of scratch. As you get fixed on drugs, that money is barely enough to cover your fixes."

PAS: Do you have regrets?

VICKI: *(long pause)* "Yeah, I have lots. Look at me. I am not a good looking chick. I am pushing 40 and think I look like an old lady or worse.

PAS: Why do you think girls turn to the streets?

VICKI: "Cash, baby. It's all about the cash and the glamour."

PAS: Glamour?

VICKI: "Didn't you see Pretty Woman? Girls are suckers for mushy shit. They think hot guys with lots of cash driving sexy cars come and take you away from here. That's total bullshit! That shit doesn't happen on the streets. You never see guys coming around here who are rich and famous. You never see expensive cars. The only expensive cars that do come here are old men looking for a quickie because their wives won't do what they want. They come looking for dirty girls. *(long pause)* Where most girls hang are shit holes. We get our asses booted out fast whenever we go to where the money is. We are looked at like rats. No one wants rodents around there. So we hang in the hole. Scum hangs around the hole. That's what you meet there...scum with money for sex or drugs."

PAS: Did you really think Richard Gere or someone like him would sweep you off your feet and save you?

VICKI: *(chuckle)* "Yeah...sort of. You know you're there to put out and guys are only there looking to get their rocks off. *(pause)* But I guess deep down you always hope or wonder when someone will save you. You want to feel successful and you want to feel wanted."

PAS: Have you ever deep down felt wanted?

VICKI: *(long reflection)* "Honestly...no. I was raised in a foster home and on the streets when I was 15. If your parents don't want you and it starts to feel like no one wants you, how can you feel wanted? *(chuckle)* You start to wonder what it means to be wanted and how that would feel."

PAS: You've done lots of drugs?

VICKI: "Yes."

PAS: Why?

VICKI: *(long stare)* "Why do you think? It's the thing to do to get you fixed for your duty. You do a lot of bad shit and there is no way you can be sober for that. You start to hate yourself. You feel like shit and think you are shit. *(long reflection)* It really numbs the hurt...from what guys do to you and what you are doing to yourself. I don't love me and no one loves me. You think after doing all the johns you do, there will be one who will be the one."

PAS: The one?

VICKI: "Yeah, the fairytale. *(with a smile)* The shit you see in the movies. It's not real, none of it. When they show broads getting beaten or killed, oh yeah, that's the real stuff. Doing lines or needles, that's the real stuff. There isn't anything pretty in this line of work."

PAS: Do you buy into the notion of "bad boys" being thrilling and fun?

VICKI: *(with a sarcastic chuckle)* "Bad boys? What's that? Guys who think they are cool and tough? Let me tell you this...If it's got the word bad in front of it, then stay the hell away! What good ever came out of bad? There are a lot of young chicks who think they are bad asses, getting all inked up and hooking up with pimp daddies. Have them come and see me 20 years from now and tell me it's all good and it was all worth it. Rude awakening!"

CHAPTER EIGHTEEN

FINAL THOUGHTS

One of the things about equality is not just that you be treated equally to a man, but that you treat yourself equally to the way you treat a man.

Marlo Thomas

I hope I have been able to provide you with new insights as to why women want what they can't have and men want what they already had. Everyone is a unique individual with different ideas, dreams, desires, and goals. When you add gender differences into the equation, the differences sometimes become so much greater.When you really think about how women and men appear to be very different, in reality they are very much alike. Both are humans made of flesh and blood. Both were born and are someday going to die. Both have feelings, laugh when they are happy and cry when they are hurt. And most importantly, both need each other.Socialization has made us who and what we are. Because of researchers and psychologists, we are better able at seeing what makes people tick. Knowing who we are and what we are is the first step. Knowing how we became the way we are is the second step, usually a more painstaking, thought invoking activity. Changing ourselves appropriately is the most difficult step. Perhaps the greatest gender difference can be seen in "change." It seems where women readily welcome change and growth, men feel more vulnerable to these threatening winds.

Men have been taught to stay the way they are. Women have been taught to evolve and change. Until we can modify existing social values and norms which encompass gender socialization, differences will continue to exist. We have come a long way over the last decade. Men are becoming more open-minded and some are accepting change more readily. In order for us to become better partners in marriages and parents to our children, we need to get along better with our mates. The best way to get along with one another is through honest and open communication.

Many people, have asked me what I think can be done to bridge gender gaps and ensure for more prosperous child-rearing in the new millennium. I believe in "grassroots" communication, which means we need to go back to the basics. Children are often told to "shut-up" or be "seen and not heard." Funny, as we become adults, we tend to communicate less with one another. In fact, parents tend to communicate even less with their own children!

Self-help books have paved a new highway into improving communication skills. Unfortunately, most of what people read becomes resigned even though they were so enthused about changing and reacting in more positive ways. Communication and relationships are like any other skill or talent. You need to practice them and dedicate your time, interest, and energies into them. If people shared the same enthusiasm about their relationships as they did about other things they focus on, there would be less marital and relational breakdowns.

I believe more "life-skill" type courses need to be implemented at the elementary and secondary school levels. Reading, writing, and arithmetic are traditionally great courses to be learned, but let's not leave out the other "R" course... Relationships! We will spend more time communicating in relationships, work, and social leisure the rest of our lives than we will solving mathematical equations, reading selected English literature, and mastering our penmanship. Children need to learn at an early age that androgyny is okay. It will enhance both the development of behaviors and personality. Only when this is done, will the largest river which separates women and men be bridged!

REFERENCES

Balswick, J.O., & Peck, C. (1971). The inexpressive male: A tragedy of American society? The Family Coordinator 20, 363-368.

Bandura, A. (1960). Relationships of family patterns to child behavior disorders (Progress report, USPHS, Project No. M-1734). Stanford, CA: Stanford University.

Bandura, A., & Huston, A. (1961). Identification as a process of incidental learning. Journal of Abnormal and Social Psychology, 63 (12), 311-318.

Beck, A.T. (1963). Thinking and depression. Archives of General Psychiatry, 9, 324-333.

Beck, A.T. (1976). Cognitive therapy and emotional disorders. New York: Internations Universities Press.

Beck, A.T. (1991). Cognitive Therapy. American Psychologist, 46, 368-375.

Bem, S.L. (1983). Gender Schema theory and its implications for child development: Raising gender aschematic children in a gender-schematic society. Signs, 8, 598-616.

Berne, E. (1964). Games people play. New York: Grove Press.

Bryson, J., & Shettel-Neuber, J. (1978). Unbalanced relationships: Who becomes jealous of whom. Cited by James Hasset in Psychology Today, 11, 26-29.

Celani, D.P. (1994). The Illusion of Love: Why the Battered Woman Returns to her Abuser. Columbia University Press.

Cooley, C.H. (1922). Human Nature and the Social Order, rev. ed. New York: Scribner's.

Devito, J.A. (1996). Messages: Building interpersonal communication skills, Third Edition. Harper Collins College Publishers.

Diagnostic and Statistical Manual of Mental Disorders, Fourth Edition (DSM-IV) American Psychological Association 1994.

Freud, S. (1905). These essays on the theory of sexuality. In Standard edition, Vol. VII, pp. 125-245. London: Hogarth Press, 1953.

Freud, S, (1913). Totem and taboo. New York. Vintage Books.

Freud, S. (1943). A general introduction to psychoanalysis. Garden City, NY; Garden City Publishing. (Originally published 1971).

Freud, S. (1953). Contributions to the psychology of love: A special type of choice objects made by men. In E. Jones (Ed.), Collected papers (Vol. 4) (pp. 192-202). London; Hogarth Press. (Originally published 1933).

Gray, J. (1992). Men are from Mars, women are from Venus: A practical guide for improving communication and getting what you want in your relationship. Harper Collins Press.

Gudykunst, W.B. (1991). Bridging differences: effective intergroup communication. Newbury Park, CA: Sage.

Hazan, C., & Shaver, P. (1987). Love conceptualized as an attachment process. Journal of Personality and Social Psychology, 52, 511-524.

Jung, C.G. (1953). The stages of life. In H. Read, M. Fordham, & G. Adler (Eds.), Collected works (Vol.2). Princeton University Press. (Original works published 1931).

Jung, C.G. (1966). Two essays on analytical psychology. In Collected Works (Vol.7). Princeton, NJ: Princeton University Press.

King, B.M. (1999). Human sexuality today: Third Edition. Prentice-Hall.

Lamb, M.E. (1986). The father's role: Cross-cultural perspectives. Hillsdale NJ: Erlbaum.

Langlois, J.H., & Downs, A.C. (1980). Mothers, fathers, and peers as socialization agents of sex-typed play behaviors in young children. Child Development, 51, 1237-1247.

Lee, J.A. (1974, October, 8). The styles of loving. Psychology Today, pp. 43-50.

Lee, J.A. (1976). The colors of love. Englewood Cliffs, NJ: Prentice Hall.

Maslow, A.H. (1968). Towards a psychology of being (2nd ed.). Princeton NJ: Van Nostrand.

McDermott, A. CNN.com, "Nicole Simpson Profile", January 19, 1995.

Messick, R.M., & Cook, K.S. (1983). Equity theory: Psychological and sociological perspectives. New York: Praeger.

Parke, R.D., & O'Leary, S.E. (1976). Father-mother-infant interaction in the newborn period: Some findings, some observations and some unresolved issues. In K.F. Roegal & J.A. Meacham (Eds.) The developing individual in a changing world: Vol. 2. Social and environmental issues (pp. 653-663). Chicago: Aldine.

Piaget, J. (1952). The origins of intelligence in children. New York: International Universities Press.

Quadagno, D., & Sprague, J. (1991). Reasons for having sex. Medical Aspects of Human Sexuality, p. 52.

Skinner, B.F. (1938). The behavior of organisms: An experimental approach. New York: Apple-Century.

Watson, J.B., 7 Rayner, R. (1920). Conditioned emotions reactions. Journal of Experimental Psychology, 3, 1-14.

Walster, E., Walster, G.W., & Berscheid, E. (1978). Equity: Theory and research. Boston: Allyn and Bacon.

Weitzman, S. (2001). Not to People Like Us. Perseus Books.

OTHER RECOMMENDED READINGS

Deborah Tannen
Gender and Discourse

John Gray
Mars and Venus Together Forever: Relationship Skills
for Lasting Love

John Bradshaw
Creating Love/ The Next Stage of Growth

Gloria Steinem
Revolution from Within: A Book of Self-Esteem

Laura C. Schlessinger
Ten Stupid Things Couples Do to Mess Up Their
Relationships

Robert H. Schuller
Self Love

Robert A. Schuller
Walking in Your Own Shoes

Jack Canfield and D.D. Watkins
Jack Canfield's Key to Living the Law of Attraction

For those interested in contacting the author for comments, questions, or speaking engagements, Peter Andrew Sacco can be reached at:

psacco1@cogeco.ca

Please visit his website at: www.petersacco.com

Your comments and opinions are greatly valued and appreciated! Thank you!

OTHER BOOKS BY THE AUTHOR

NON-FICTION

What's Your Anger Type?

Breast Envy (co-authored with Dr. Debra Laino, Sex Therapist)

 Penis Envy

The Madonna Complex (co-authored with Dr. Debra Laino, Sex Therapist)

Fast Food Dating, Your 2 Cents!

CPSIA information can be obtained
at www.ICGtesting.com
Printed in the USA
LVHW031748041219
639426LV00001B/27/P